FRACTURED MEMORIES

Because Demented People Need Love, Too

EMILY PAGE

Contents

Prologue

The Eulogy

A reading from the Book of Nick:

A guy who works in an aquarium gets summoned by his boss, who is looking very worried. She says to him, "I've just been by the dolphin tank, and they're feeling very amorous. They're doing all sorts of things to each other. And the trouble is that, in less than an hour, we've got three busloads of second graders coming. We can't have them watching those naughty dolphins. Now, there's only one thing that acts as an anti-aphrodisiac for dolphins, and that's the meat of baby seagulls. So I want you to go down to the seashore, catch yourself some baby seagulls, and hurry back. But be careful, a lion escaped from the zoo this morning, and though he was heavily sedated, he still might be dangerous." So the guy takes a shortcut through the forest to the seashore. He gets some baby seagulls, and he's walking back through the forest when he sees the lion, and it is lying across the path directly in front of him. It's too late to run away, and the feline does seem very placid, so, summoning his courage, he steps across the lion. Nothing happens, and with much relief, the guy resumes his journey, when all of a sudden, a policeman steps out of the forest and grabs the guy and says to him, "You're under arrest." The guy can't believe it and asks the officer what the charge is. The policeman says, "Transporting young gulls across a sedate lion for immoral porpoises."

As pieces of my dad have slipped away over the last few years, I've had plenty of time to reflect on what we've been losing and what I've been missing. Here are just a few: I miss dancing with my dad – at my high school's traditional parent-child dance for senior prom, at my wedding, around the dinner table with the music turned up so loud the cats went running. I'm going to miss his easy laugh when we played the game where we tried to get the worst songs stuck in each other's head, or when we could only speak in song titles or lyrics. I miss hiking in the woods with him, talking about everything that worried or thrilled me, and how he took me so seriously, even when I was just a kid. I miss walking the train tracks with him, or laughing at Miss Piggy. I miss hearing him snoring down the hall, and late-night sessions in high school, laughing at televangelists when neither of us could sleep. I miss throwing rocks and playing "pooh sticks" and "Dad the human jungle gym." I miss flattening pennies on the railroad tracks, or leaving pennies, head-side up, in random places for strangers to find and saying, "This is going to make someone verrrrrrry happy!" I miss the handwriting that looked like he should have been a doctor. I miss the way he embraced my friends, assuming that if I loved them, he loved them. I miss imitating *Beyond the Fringe* and Jonathan and Darlene records with him. I miss our easy shorthand. I miss the way he looked at me when I sang. I miss how he'd roughhouse and snuggle with the kitties. I miss his Christmas newsletter. I miss his radio show. I miss watching his band at First Night Virginia and other gigs. I miss hearing him practicing to Jamey Aebersold records in the background while I read. I even miss him farting and saying someone must have stepped on a frog.

I loved his firm belief in equal rights for everyone – women, men, black, white, gay, straight. I love that he taught me to stand up for what I believe in and to find a way to make a living doing what I love. He taught me to seek my own truth and not just accept what I'm told. He taught me that it's okay to be a star, but to never forget that there are millions of other stars out there waiting for someone to recognize them for what they are – to treat people as if they too are important, special, and full of light. He taught me that life is a process and no decision is final, that we constantly choose and get to change course and reshape our lives. He taught me to clap on the two and the four, and to relish the ridiculous. He taught me to say I love you early and often, and mean it.

In *Fugitive Pieces*, Anne Michaels wrote, "The dead are everywhere but the ground." She's right. My dad is in that distant train whistle. He's in every lucky penny you find. He's in your favorite jazz riff or dirty joke.

In the last fifteen to twenty years, my dad wasn't what you would call a religious man, but he was definitely spiritual. He looked for meaning in life, and I think he found it. The meaning in all of this, in all of you, is friendship, love. He was generous and loyal to a fault and loved each of his friends deeply. And you've returned that love tenfold. The cards and phone calls and gifts that you sent when he was diagnosed, when he had his final radio show, and when he was admitted into the dementia unit, the rides you offered to town when he had to stop driving, the visits you made to see him in the dementia unit, all of it, was staggeringly kind. The staff at the facility was, frankly, amazed at the outpouring of love they saw from his friends and family on a daily basis. I think it helped them see who he had been before the disease. And when I would start to forget who my father had been, losing him in who he had become as a result of the dementia, those cards and such would remind me of why I still loved him so fiercely – why I still *love* him so fiercely.

So, on his behalf, thank you for wholeheartedly returning his love.

PART I

Chapter One

Who He Was

Let me start by saying that my dad was The Best Dad Ever. No, really. You can tell me all the stories you want about how awesome your dad is, but you will never convince me that yours is even close to as great as mine. I mean it. Quit talking all that craziness. My dad was like a cupcake inside an ice cream cake inside a regular cake – basically he was the turducken of desserts. This is not to say that he was edible, just that he was fanfreakingtastic. My dad was so awesome that, when he was diagnosed with frontotemporal dementia at the age of sixty-five, he started saying to people who asked how he was doing, "Not bad for a demented guy." Beat that. We can talk more later about all the other ways my dad is better than your dad, but for now, I'm going to give you a little of his backstory.

Born Nicholas Allen Page in Indianapolis in 1942 to Dr. Irvine Heinly Page and Beatrice Allen Page, my father grew up mostly in Cleveland. His family spent summers on Cape Cod in Hyannis Port, where his brother and friends learned to sail, and where he claimed to learn to "be ballast." He loved to pedal his bike down to the rail yard and greet the incoming engineers, and eventually managed to talk them all into hauling his bike up into the cab to ride into the yard. He was obsessed with trains, and, as a child, had an entire room in his home devoted to model trains.

He never outgrew the obsession, and would take family and friends on long train-chasing expeditions. We'd load the kitties into a VW camper and camp by the tracks, where he'd take endless photos and slides of the passing trains. He knew all the train schedules by heart, so in college, all his friends would just ask him what their options were if they needed to take a train somewhere. In Vietnam, he talked another friend into sneaking off base to try to pry the front plate off of an abandoned train (they failed, by the way, because they hadn't brought any tools along, but the upside was that they weren't captured or killed by the enemy, so there's that…). Dad convinced Mom that they should buy land with train tracks running through it, and hired an architect with the last name Train to build an addition to the house they had already built, complete with tons of windows facing the tracks, and which also bore a striking resemblance to a train station. The wall in their bedroom was built at an angle so that their bed faced out toward the tracks, and there was a light switch by the headboard that my dad (an insomniac) could turn on at night to light up the tracks when a train came through. They named the twenty-five acres of land they bought High Green, because that's the term for the signal the engineers get when it's safe to proceed. Of course, the authorities thought it was code for "the new people must be growing marijuana" and would send helicopters circling overhead to check our woods. We had scanners in every room of the house so we'd know when a train was coming and could run to the porch to wave as it passed. When trains would pause at our railroad crossing, Dad would hike down and chat them up. So they started saying hi to him over the scanner as they passed by. There were model trains and train whistles displayed in the built-in bookshelves. He had records of train sounds, videos of trains, and he bought a digital recorder so he could make recordings himself of the trains as they chugged by. Every night after dinner, we'd walk the tracks, practicing our balancing skills (I would have been great as a gymnast on the balance beam – feel free to call me Nadia), and talking about our days. We put coins on the track for the trains to flatten as they passed and then we'd have to hunt them down. He rebuilt an entire locomotive engine in our yard. Okay, that last one was a lie, but the rest is true. So you get the idea. Train buff, nut, loon.

Train Watching 48" x 36" acrylic, ink, and paper on board

My dad went to Wake Forest University, from which he graduated with a degree in political science, which was almost as practical as my art degree. Because he had been in ROTC in college, when he graduated he went to Vietnam, where he became a first lieutenant (when we applied to move my dad into a dementia care facility many years later, the intake form asked if he'd been in the military and what his rank was, so we wrote that he'd been a first lieutenant. Later, the facility staff wrote in his bio that he had been *the* first lieutenant in Vietnam) in military intelligence – a term he always joked was an oxymoron. In Vietnam, Dad had a monkey that hated women and thus seriously hampered his dating life. He'd bring a date to his barracks and the monkey (who may have been named Monkey Mouse) would hurl feces at her. One day, the monkey disappeared and a nearby restaurant advertised monkey on the menu.

Dad did not believe in the war, so upon his return, he grew a long, dirty-hippy beard and joined the protest movement, wearing his combat fatigues every day and lying down in the street to protest. He was a man of conscience. His best friend was killed in Vietnam, which was something I think my dad never really got over. Growing up, I tried asking questions about the time he served in the army, but he was fairly reticent. It wasn't until the dementia started that he began talking to me about his experiences. He got shot at in helicopters on recon missions and suffered from PTSD when he returned to the States, though it wasn't recognized at the time. He told me that if he heard a car backfire outside his apartment in Chicago, he'd dive under the bed. I still have one of his shirts from Vietnam, and it's a source of comfort for me. I'm proud that my dad had the courage to serve, and that he also had the courage when he came back to stand up and say that what was happening over there wasn't right. I love that he didn't lose his humanity, and did therapy in seminary that no doubt helped him deal with the PTSD and the loss of his best friend, thus enabling him to move on. I love that he remained loyal to that friend's family, even when that had to be painful at times. I love that he didn't get brainwashed into thinking that the military was only ever right, nor that it was only ever wrong.

Fatigues 6" x 6" oil on canvas

In part because of pressure from his parents, he became a stockbroker in Cleveland, but hated it and decided to go to Chicago Theological Seminary for his masters of divinity. There, he met the woman of his dreams, Jane Fonda. Just kidding. He met the *other* woman of his dreams: my mom. Mom was working at the school and dating one of the professors, who, she says, basically pawned her off on Dad. But that turned out to be a very good thing, and before long, he was smitten. They started dating, moved in together, and got a couple cats that they named "I" and "Thou" (after the title of a Martin Buber book because, apparently, they were smart or something). But when Dad graduated, Mom, who was tired of central Illinois, wanted to get her master's degree, as well, and got into the Pacific School of Religion in California. Not wanting to break up the cats, they decided to get married. I mean, can you think of a better reason than that? Being a dirty hippy herself, Mom made her own "autumn rust" colored wedding dress. Dad wore a paisley shirt, a seersucker jacket, a striped tie, and bell-bottoms. Mom talked him out of wearing his combat boots for the special occasion. I have a fantastic photo of the two of them coming out of the church and Dad has both hands raised with his fingers in V's, imitating Nixon. Totally appropriate for your wedding photo, right?

My parents bought a house in Berkeley, and not long after, I popped out of my poor mother. I tried my best to kill her during childbirth, but luckily, she's a badass and she survived. Even though I looked like an Inuit when I first came out, and I have to wonder if my father worried that I wasn't actually his, I quickly wrapped Dad around my little finger. Lest you, dear reader, worry, in no time at all I looked disturbingly like him – to the point that I donned his clothes, glasses, and a fake beard as a kid to be him for Halloween one year. In California, Mom got her masters of divinity and Dad got a certificate in alcohol and drug abuse counseling and worked in several programs in the Bay Area.

Eventually, my parents decided that they were tired of the earthquakes, droughts and fires, and of the lack of seasons and lightning bugs, and decided it was time to move east. Kind of accidentally on purpose, they ended up picking Charlottesville, VA. They bought a home with the intention of living in it, renovating it, then flipping it, but fell in love with the house once they'd renovated it, so stayed there. It was right in the delightful fraternity-row part of town, which, when they'd visited it, had been quiet and charming because it was in the middle of summer and the students were gone. Then the students came back, and as we drove through our neighborhood on our way to move into our new home, little six-year-old me exclaimed in awe, "The girls are having a party! The boys are having a party! Everyone's having a party!" Yep, nothing gets past Captain Obvious here. Our house was right next door to a sorority, and late at night, the drunken guys who were always visiting would pee into our yard. So Dad finally got fed up and hid in the bushes with a hose and sprayed them down when they whipped out their willies. After not too many years, my parents started wanting to escape the weekend party noise, so they bought property (which we later found out was ancestral territory) about twenty minutes south of town in the GFW (god forsaken wilderness) and we'd camp there on weekends. Then they built a screened porch because of the vampiric mosquitos and ticks, along with an outhouse. Tired of my whining, they built a small house next. And I do mean that *they* built it, board by board. And finally, right about the time that I started to get interested in the young men ~~stumbling~~ strolling past our house, they hired an architect to build a large addition to the house so that we could live there permanently.

At age forty, my dad decided that, damn it, he wanted to do what he really wanted to do, and that was return to music, specifically, jazz. He had played clarinet and saxophone in high school, college, and Vietnam, but his efforts at being a responsible adult led him to abandon music for a while. And now he wanted to start that up again, so he began messing around with other musician friends, forming a band of sorts and calling themselves "The Windbreakers." At the end of a set, they'd turn away from the audience, bend over, and honk their horns. They were classy like that. My mom said this story was apocryphal (which I had to look up), but I have a distinct memory of this happening at my mom's fortieth birthday party, which may actually have been the only gig they ever played. He then started a band called The Red Hot Smoothies, and they played gigs for twenty-something years around Virginia.

Sax 6" x 6" oil on canvas

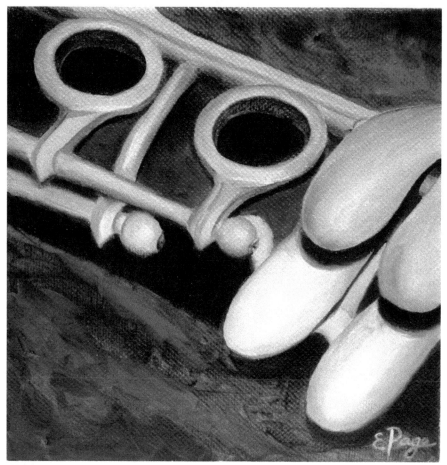
Clarinet 6" x 6" oil on canvas

He also had a radio show for ten years called *Nick @ Nine* – "Monday morning jazz to make you feel good." He played primarily swing bands and a few vocalists, and I got to cohost with him several times when I'd come to visit after I graduated from college. He also hosted a show with several other deejays called *New Month, New Music*, where they'd preview new albums and then argue about whether the music was any good or should be hurled off a cliff into a fiery ravine full of venomous snakes.

A couple other random things you should know about him: He had an exuberant walk. He loved being out in nature and walking. It's like all the joy bubbled up and made him bounce on his toes when he walked. He loved a good Scotch. Every day at five p.m., he and my mom would have a Scotch and he and a good family friend used to trade bottles of good Scotch for Christmas. He adored kitties. We had one cat that was absolutely crazy about him and wanted to be on him at all times. We'd turn the music way up and dance around the dining room, and the other cats all went flying, but this cat, Obie, would let him hold her while he bounced around, and she'd just look up at him lovingly the whole time. While he practiced the clarinet and the saxophone, she'd drape herself over his shoulders. When it was time for a nap, she'd curl up on his chest and purr into his face.

Obie 6" x 6" oil on canvas

Scotch 6" x 6" oil on canvas

As a husband, he was devoted. He turned down gigs that would have required him to spend nights away from home because he couldn't bear to be apart from my mom. He loved her madly. She was his best friend and they were a good team. The only times I remember them fighting were when they were building or renovating a house. My dad would cut a board without measuring and so would get it wrong, and my mom would measure twelve times and never get to cutting. But other than that, they were pretty harmonious. Of course, they argued about things all couples argue about, but they very clearly loved and respected each other.

Then there was his role as my dad. As mentioned at the start, he was the best. The best. THE. BEST. When I was little, he was so playful with me. On the long car rides around the country chasing trains, he'd entertain me by making up stories with me – absurd stories about blue rocks and poop and ducks "who stepped in it." He made up a bedtime story for me about a little girl named Emily who was camping with her family and in the middle of the night woke her parents up to tell them that she heard something outside. Her daddy didn't believe her, but eventually she wore him down and he went outside to investigate. There, he discovered a little baby bunny who was "cold, hungry, tired, aaaaand wet." Long story short, the little girl saves the bunny and all live happily ever after. He told me that story repeatedly, always including the tag line that the bunny was cold, hungry, tired, aaaaand wet. Years later, when the dementia had firmly taken hold of his ability to talk, I could say "cold, hungry, tired," and he'd still finish "aaaaand wet."

My dad loved being a father. He was a strong feminist, and was very concerned that he not treat me like a girly girl. He discouraged crying. We'd go throw rocks in the river while camping. I had my own toy train set. He and my mom shared cooking and cleaning duties. It was an egalitarian household. I remember when *Beauty and the Beast* came out, he sat me down to remind me that if I met a beast, no amount of love was going to change him. But he also let me foster my girly side. He sat patiently while I put barrettes in his hair and blush on his cheeks. He did his best to protect his groin when I decided to use him as a human jungle gym and slide down him over and over and over. When I was in high school, we were both insomniacs, so we'd get up and make scrambled eggs and hash browns and laugh at the late night televangelists with their crazy eighties hair. After dinner, we went for walks on the tracks, and I'd talk about everything that ever occurred to me, and he did his best to treat me like my revelations were as profound as I thought they were. He took me out to a muddy field to teach me how to drive a truck and slide around in the mud while not overcorrecting. He got me music lessons on the piano and the flute as a kid, and managed not to act too disappointed when I wouldn't practice and gave them up. And later, as a teenager, he got me voice lessons with a fantastic jazz singer he knew when I expressed an interest. He shared the music he loved with me. We'd listen to the Coasters and Louis Prima when I was a kid, and he'd beam when I'd sing the sax solos. Later, he'd beam when I sang along with Ella Fitzgerald, Sarah

Vaughan, and Carmen McRae. He bought me my first CD: Beethoven, and later stocked my music collection with jazz of all kinds. My high school had a tradition that for senior prom, the parents attended for the first song, and father-daughter and mother-son duos danced. My dad and I practiced in our living room, so when the time came, ninety-nine percent of the duos looked pathetic, but Dad and I waltzed grandly around the room. If we could have, we would have done a mic drop, 'cause BOOM, y'all, we owned that shit. When I got married, his band played for my wedding, and I have a fantastic picture of Sebastian and me dancing, with my dad playing the saxophone in the background, watching over us. That's what my parents were so spectacular at: watching over me from a safe distance; allowing me to try things and fail, and glowing with me when I succeeded. My mom and I had a great relationship. We loved each other, rarely fought, enjoyed shopping trips and horseback riding together. She let me cry when I needed to. She did crafts with me and taught me how to use a curling iron. But my dad and I were the stars. We cracked each other up, speaking in silly accents, or only speaking in song lyrics, or getting into pun wars. We were two peas in a pod.

And all of that was great, but what set him apart from the rest of the world were two things: First, he was *hilarious*. Seriously…or comically…or, oh hell, I don't know. The guy was funny – like, make-you-squirt-soda-out-of-your-nose funny. Painfully funny. He loved a dirty joke. He reveled in the absurd. To him, silliness was a thing of beauty. He could have been a Muppet (one of the musicians, of course). When two gay male friends had a party just for their favorite ladies in town, Dad donned a pink dress and blonde wig so he could attend (let me tell you, his beard did not make him the most attractive female).

Miss Piggy 6" x 6" oil on canvas

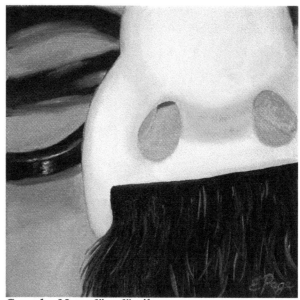
Groucho Nose 6" x 6" oil on canvas

While he, like many members of our family, suffered from depression, it was his mission in life to make people laugh. At his funeral, people said repeatedly how easily he laughed and could make them laugh, even in the worst situations. They also said repeatedly how he'd mentored people, which leads me to the other thing that set him apart: he made you feel special. When he was talking with you about anything even vaguely serious, he was all ears. Insightful, caring, helpful, you just knew that what you had to say was important, whether you were a peer or a kid. There aren't a lot of people in the world who are good listeners. But my dad knew that there was something inside just about everybody worthy of love, and he looked for it and helped you see it in yourself. He and a female friend who was a tough nut and pretty caustic used to joke that "bitches need love, too." He tried to show people how loved they were, even when they didn't love themselves.

And all of that is what made my dad my best friend. We had the same sense of humor, the same taste in music, the same desire to please people. We could make each other crack up with just a look. I shared everything with him – boy troubles, school troubles, my depression, my dreams for my future. His father had not been the most affectionate man, and my dad made a conscious decision that he wasn't going to do that with me. I got hugs galore. He paid attention to me. He treated me like I wasn't as irrational as I probably was most of the time. He expected respect and reciprocated it. Around the time most kids started to think their parents were trying to ruin their lives by being so utterly uncool, I was busy introducing all of my friends to mine. My mom and I got along very well and loved each other deeply, but my dad and I were *it*. I didn't just look like him, I thought like him. We just…*got* each other.

And then came the dementia.

Chapter Two

Early Signs, Or, My Dad's Getting Weird…er

The changes were subtle at first: misplacing things, locking keys in the car, difficulty with the computer, paying for things with credit card instead of cash. He'd started a new job selling cars and was a top performer, but when the economy dipped, he started getting stressed, so it was easy to attribute some of the changes my husband and I were seeing to that stress. Dad had started to seem a little distracted, and he was quieter on the phone. I was living in Florida, and my parents and I talked regularly on the phone, and usually my mom was the quieter of the two, but that had started to change some. Valuable insights that I depended on slowed. But so many things, like him misplacing things, just seemed like things that were already a part of his personality, but to the nth degree. It's a daily battle for me to not ~~murder my husband's face off~~ yell at my husband when he puts the dishes in the wrong place or doesn't replace the cap on the toothpaste tube, and the stuff my dad was doing was very much like that: just *guy* stuff (Yes, I know that's a sexist statement. Sue me. Wait, no, please don't sue me. I take it back. It's just the stuff that the guys in *my* life do. Not all guys. I know that other guys are miraculous organizers and are made of rainbow bunny-rabbit kisses and are like Mary Poppins – practically perfect in every way).

As early as 2006, I think the changes were starting to take place; we just didn't realize it at the time. Being the highly functioning, intelligent person that he was, my father was able to mask and compensate for most inadequacies. Around that time, I noticed that my dad had started drinking more than I'd seen before. Not that he was drinking heavily or ever got *drunk* drunk, but I thought he was getting a little tipsy sometimes, which was uncharacteristic, given his prior work as an alcohol and drug abuse counselor. Always a very socially adept person, a couple times, after a couple drinks, he asked my friends questions that were a little uncomfortable or put them on the spot, like, "So why aren't you two a couple?" Awkward.

My dad actually developed a bleeding ulcer and, not long after, decided that selling cars was no longer the thing for him and that it was time to retire. We all assumed he would improve once the stress of the job was eliminated. But the distraction that my husband, Sebastian, and I had noticed did not improve. When my parents came down to visit us in Florida in 2008, we went to our favorite buffet. You'd go through the salad bar and load up, then pay at the register, and find a seat and chow down. When your plate was clean, you'd hit the rest of the foods laid out in the dining area's buffet line. As usual, we went through the salad bar and paid, then grabbed a seat and started ~~shoving massive quantities~~

of food down our gullets eating…except that Dad never found his way to our table. After several minutes, he was nowhere to be seen. I found him on the opposite end of the restaurant eating happily, oblivious to the fact that he was eating alone. We all laughed it off, but when my parents left to head back to Virginia, Sebastian and I both commented to each other that something seemed, well, *off*. Still, we didn't say anything to my parents because we weren't sure how to bring it up.

My parents ended up being the ones to say something to us first. Mom had noticed a lot of the same changes, and also said that Dad had been agitated, prone to tears and angry outbursts. Awhile back, Dad had been to his primary-care physician, who said that it was a normal part of aging. Again, as a very intelligent person, he was able to compensate. But when things seemed to worsen, Dad returned to his physician and was referred to a neurologist at the University of Virginia for more testing. They were awaiting the results when they called to tell me. Mom attended the testing with him and was shocked at the simple things he couldn't do, like tell time on a clock. If asked to explain a saying like, "There's no use crying over spilled milk," he wasn't able to explain what it meant beyond the literal meaning.

It wasn't until the end of January 2009 that the appointment to get the results finally arrived. I flew home so that I could hear firsthand what the doctor had to say. The night before had been full of worry. The weather forecast predicted snow overnight, and our appointment was scheduled for very early the next morning so that I could catch my flight back to Florida that afternoon. Since we lived in the GFW, the rural roads didn't get plowed. Instead, we and our neighbors who owned tractors would plow the sections of the road in front of our properties, but getting to the city roads was a dicey endeavor. We considered driving into town that night and getting a hotel room, but decided to take our chances. Luckily, the snow was light and we made it safely to the doctor's office on time. Given what my mom had seen when my dad was being tested, we knew something was very wrong, but hearing the results was shocking, nonetheless. I remember thinking that the tech delivering the results to us was impossibly young to be giving such devastating news.

At age sixty-five, my dad was in the early stages of frontotemporal dementia (FTD), which is the progressive cell degeneration of the brain's frontal and temporal lobes. Not being an expert here, I'm going to break it down as simply as I can. There are three different subtypes that fall under FTD: primary progressive aphasia (basically, difficulty with speech), movement or muscle dysfunction (which can happen with or without the other two types of FTD), and behavior variant frontotemporal dementia (bvFTD). This last one is what Dad had. According to the Alzheimer's Association, "This condition is characterized by prominent changes in personality, interpersonal relationships, and conduct that often occur in people in their 50s and 60s, but can develop as early as their 20s or as late as their 80s. In bvFTD, the nerve cell loss is most prominent in areas that control conduct, judgment, empathy, and foresight, among other abilities." All of that fit with the behavior changes we'd been seeing. We, of course, had a lot of questions, which the doctors answered, but many questions I didn't want to ask in front of my father.

By the day that he received the diagnosis, I had seen my father cry only three times: once when our cat Fat Cat died, once when our cat Persi died, and once when he arrived to the scene of a pretty horrible car accident from which I emerged with only minor injuries. He had come from a long line of relative stoics, of whom he was by far the most emotive. He had raised me not to cry, though I was a ~~giant ball of weepiness~~ considerably less skilled at suppressing my tears.

Nevertheless, as we walked from the neurologist's office to the car, his shoulders began to shake. I stood there in the cold Virginia air with wet snow seeping into my sneakers and heart and felt utterly helpless. In that moment, I ceased playing the role of daughter to him, and began the role of caretaker. After we stood in the parking lot wrapped in a three-person hug and weeping, my parents took me to the airport where I boarded a flight back to Florida, still reeling from the news. I sat on the plane and looked out the window and fought to catch my breath. I had written the words "frontotemporal dementia" on a piece of paper, and I kept reading it over and over and trying to make sense of what the doctors had told us. It didn't seem real.

When I got home, I, of course, got online and started researching the disease. What I saw was not good. Asshole internet, which so very often lies, refused to lie to me that night. The symptoms all matched: odd social behavior (disinhibition), inability to make changes or follow complicated instructions, heightened emotion, depression. Treatment was aimed at managing symptoms, not slowing or stopping the disease. There were no medications for that. Prognosis: death two to ten years after diagnosis, probably from pneumonia after aspirating food because of muscle failure.

Shock does not even begin to describe what I was feeling. My grandparents, on both sides of my family, lived to at least ninety years old. My grandfathers both died without developing senility, and my grandmothers didn't show signs until into their nineties. Of all the things that I thought would afflict my parents or me, dementia was not one of them. And dementia at the age of sixty-five (and likely even younger, since we'd been seeing signs for a couple years)? Not possible.

I talked to my parents the next day, and they had done the same thing I had: they'd done research online and were devastated. Two to ten years. Two to ten years. Two to ten years. Talking to them on the phone was so hard, because we were all crying but couldn't hold each other for comfort. My dad said he was terrified of ending up drooling in his shoe in a closet. I remember telling my dad not to do anything stupid or noble (depending on your perspective) like committing suicide to save us from having to care for him. I was truly scared that that was a possibility. I didn't want to lose any time I could have with him, regardless of his condition – not that I could even begin to comprehend what his condition would someday become.

My parents made an appointment for my dad to start counseling with Dr. Carol Manning at the Memory Disorders Clinic at UVA. He also started several prescriptions to help manage his agitation. And thus, our lives on the other side of the diagnosis began.

Dad immediately stopped drinking any alcohol, afraid that it would make things worse. He continued to do his radio show, but needed help from other deejays to run the soundboard because it was too confusing for him to keep everything straight. He cooked less because following a recipe was too hard for him. He gave control of his band to one of the other musicians.

He continued to drive until a fellow deejay rode in the car with him to go to lunch, and then emailed us that Dad wasn't able to recognize a handicap-only parking sign. At that point, my parents made an appointment to have him evaluated at the Wilson Workforce and Rehabilitation Center. He got only partway through the testing and they said he was a danger behind the wheel, so he immediately turned his driver's license in. While he had loved cars and driving his whole life (when he was a teen but too young to get a license, he bought a car to fix up and would gun it up and down the driveway repeatedly), he understood very clearly that he could hurt someone if he continued to drive. I've heard so many stories over the years of people with dementia fighting their families about wanting to continue driving, and I am so incredibly grateful that we didn't have that battle. Dad was so gracious about it. His first priority was not harming anyone else. But ceasing driving when they lived twenty minutes south of town presented a special challenge. He and Mom had to coordinate their schedules for anything that required heading to town. So, if Mom had a horseback-riding lesson at a stable even farther south at the same time that Dad wanted to go to his yoga class, someone had to give in. Luckily, friends that also lived in the GFW stepped in to help out and offer rides. Other friends who didn't live in the GFW went out of their way to drive him home.

For the first few months, things progressed relatively slowly, but I started to hear more and more frustration in my mom's voice. It was clear that Dad was driving her crazy with what she called "temper tantrums" and generally annoying behavior. Things like him reaching over and taking food off of her plate without asking, or trying to clean the wood floors (and his shoes, and the car) with a piece of steel wool, or obsessively needing to pick up trash from the side of the road – things that would drive you batshit crazy if anyone did them, and are particularly annoying when your spouse is the one doing them. You can't get distance from the behavior because you *live* with it. But when I talked to my mom and dad,

I couldn't understand what was so horrible. Yeah, Dad seemed a little scattered, but it wasn't terrible, and I kind of thought that Mom might be exaggerating a little bit. She was not prone to hyperbole, so I'm not sure why I thought that, but I guess I just wasn't hearing it in my limited interactions on the phone.

Then my mom needed to go check on her own mother, who was in her late nineties and lived on her own in Chicago, and traveling with Dad had gotten really tough. The last time she had taken him with her, he was really agitated flying, and he got lost in the retirement community where my grandmother lived. So, I agreed to come up for four days to "dadsit."

The first couple of days were fairly easy, and I really did think that my mom was making a bigger deal out of things than necessary. She had made it seem like a lot of work to keep up with him. Then we hit day three. I had made plans with a friend to come to our house for dinner, so Dad and I went to the grocery store. One of the ways that Dad's disease manifested was the compulsive need to hoard food items. So every time he went to the grocery store he wanted to buy flavored fizzy water and gum, regardless of how much of each he already had at home. I didn't know that yet. I went to the poultry section to get some chicken, and in the twenty-three seconds that I had my back turned to him, my dad disappeared. I was like one of those frantic mothers tearing through the store looking for their toddler who'd wandered off. My family has a tradition of whistling for each other when we get separated in the store so we can find each other again, so I was racing up and down the aisles whistling like a deranged bird while people gave me odd looks as I flew past. I finally found him in the flavored-water aisle, piling bottles upon bottles up in his arms. When I told him that he already had plenty of flavored water at home so he couldn't buy those, he pitched a fit. Temper tantrum, indeed. He was like a psychotic five year old, stomping his feet and yanking the bottles back from me as I tried to put them back on the shelf, and screaming at me, "But I WANT it!!" As I mentioned before, when everyone else was busy being mortified in their teen years by the things their parents did, I was proud to introduce my parents to my friends. In that moment, my dad made up for all the years I got off easy. It was *so* embarrassing. And what do you do in that situation? If he had been a kid, I could have picked him up and dragged him out of the store. I could have put him in a time out. I could have bribed him with candy. I could have slipped him some brandy (clearly, I shouldn't be a parent). But there wasn't much I could do. Reasoning with him didn't help. I finally compromised and let him buy one bottle, but he was furious with me.

He calmed down on the ride home. It was about two p.m. when we got home, and we started unpacking the groceries we'd bought. I went downstairs to put something in the deep freezer, and by the time I got back up, Dad had taken two frozen chicken breasts and plopped them on a frying pan on high heat to cook them for our dinner that was supposed to be at around six p.m. Aaaaand, dinner was now ruined. It's amazing how much trouble one man can get into in only twenty-three seconds. When I tried to explain why that wasn't the best thing to do, he just could not understand what the hell I was talking about and, again, got very upset with me for "blocking" him. I began to see what Mom was facing on a daily basis. She had not been exaggerating.

It's common for friends and family to underestimate just how hard being a caregiver to someone with dementia is, particularly in the early stages where the demented person is better able to cope and cover their disability. One can start to feel like they're going mad just with the daily frustrations of trying to find items the person they're caring for has misplaced. If they're still very mobile, like my dad, they require constant watching, because they're likely to do something "helpful" like touch up your shoes by spray painting them; or they'll use a dishcloth as a hot pad and catch the fringed edge on fire when lifting the tea kettle off of a gas burner…three times; or wander off into the adjacent woods and get lost on the trail they've walked a thousand times before. I've heard from several caregivers who've asked their adult kids to help only to be told, and I'm quoting here, "We don't do that." I'm convinced it's because those kids just really don't have any idea how utterly exhausting it is. Until you've lived with dementia, you can't fully understand how stressful it is.

For anyone reading this who has a parent, loved one, or friend with dementia who is being cared for by another family member, offer to house/adult sit for a couple days. This serves a couple purposes: it will give the caregiver a much needed break, and it will give you a much better picture of what daily life is like for the caregiver. If you can't offer a full two days, offer whatever you can – even if it's just an afternoon. It will keep the caregiver that much closer to the safe side of the sanity line.

Chapter 3

Our Year In Provence (I Wish)

My dadsitting adventure made it crystal clear that Mom was, indeed, struggling to care for Dad on her own. When I got back from the trip, Sebastian and I agreed that she needed help. Given how tight-knit my family was, the most obvious solution was for us to move up there to pitch in. We put our house in Florida on the market and prepared for the move. Several months later, it was clear that the house wasn't going to sell any time soon and my mother was getting desperate, so we found renters for the Florida house and moved up.

If I'm being honest, I don't remember most of the year we spent living with my parents. It was horrible, and I've blocked a lot of it out. Living together as adults shifted the family dynamics, and everyone was fighting. It was a time of reeling, when angry words tore from our mouths and hurtled toward one another. My husband was still coping with the death of his mother the prior year and now with living with his in-laws, my mom was coping with becoming a parent to her husband and trying to keep her home in order while trying to make sure her own mother was okay out in Chicago, and my father was dealing with having three people telling him what he could and could not do. I found myself bouncing between the three of them trying to please everyone but actually pleasing no one. We were all in pain and needed to be selfish, but felt guilty taking any time for ourselves while resenting it when anyone else actually did take any time for his or her self. We drafted a schedule so that we all had shifts watching my dad. We were jealous of each other's time away and regularly accused each other of taking more than our fair share. I began having panic attacks, the first one so bad that we called EMS. We did some family counseling with Dr. Manning, and we joined a support group for people with early stage dementia and their caregivers through the Alzheimer's Association, and I did some counseling on my own. All of that kept us from killing each other, but just barely. It was a year of desperation and frustration.

One of the ways my dad's dementia manifested was that he got agitated if he didn't have something to do. You'd give him a task and fifteen seconds later, he was ready for whatever was next. Because dementia demands so much time and energy and thought from the caregivers, I have decided to rename it "demandtia." Keeping Dad safely occupied was a challenge. In our first few months, he was competent to get himself dressed and fed breakfast. Then one of us would drive him to town for his yoga class. We usually followed that with lunch at our favorite bagel shop, and perhaps some grocery shopping while we were in town. Then it was back home where we'd struggle to find enough things for him to do. We started coloring in coloring books with him, though his attention span made that a pretty short-lived activity. In the summer months, we'd supervise him swimming, or have him practice his sax or clarinet, but each activity lasted only a few minutes before he was bored with it and wanted to be entertained with something else. He had a hard time following a story, so reading was no longer an option. He couldn't sit still long enough to watch a movie. We had a stinkbug and lady-bug infestation, and he would constantly make us pause the movie so he could get up off of the sofa to run around swatting at them or trying to vacuum them up, which made the whole house smell like cilantro (I swear, that's what stinkbugs smell like, which is why I don't eat cilantro) every time we vacuumed. One day, I looked outside and he was running around the yard with a flyswatter trying to kill every last one of them before they could come in the house. A few days later, I saw him outside again, this time with the vacuum trying to suck them up before they could come inside. Secretly, I cheered him on. Plus it was keeping him somewhat safely occupied. Common sense was out the door, so cleaning the truck with steel wool (clearly, he loved cleaning with steel wool) made perfect sense. When the cats cornered and were playing with a still-living mouse in my parents' third-floor bedroom, he scooped it up and tossed it out the window, exclaiming, "I saved it!" Or, you know, *you just hurled it out a third floor window to its death.*

For some reason, he loved picking up trash from the side of the road in front of our property and our neighbors' properties, and he loved going to the dump to deposit the garbage and the recycling (there was no trash pickup service in the GFW). It was a compulsion, like hoarding gum and fizzy water. He couldn't be trusted to be on the side of the road on his own, so that would mean one of us would have to go out there to supervise, even if it was ninety degrees in the shade. And if left up to him, he'd gather the trash several times a day (even though there wasn't much after he'd *just* picked it up) and have us drive him to the dump. It was getting ridiculous, so Dr. Manning suggested we set rules for when he was allowed to do a trash/recycling run. We chose two days a week, and he was mostly okay with that, though sometimes he struggled to understand that if it wasn't Tuesday, it wasn't trash day, and he'd get irate with us for blocking him. One afternoon, my husband was driving him home from town and Dad insisted that he take him to the dump. Sebastian tried to explain that the dump wasn't open that day and that, even if it was, it wasn't a day we normally went. My father genteelly responded by telling Sebastian to fuck himself. My husband saw red. It's one thing to know on an intellectual level that it's the disease talking. It's another to keep yourself from feeling brutally attacked when you've turned your life upside down to care for the person attacking you. Sebastian has always had a strained relationship with his own father, but he and my dad got along amazingly well. Sebastian really looked up to my dad and felt like he'd finally gotten the father figure he'd always wanted, and now he was losing him and feeling rejected by him. He managed to restrain himself from punching Dad's teeth down his throat, but he did tell him how much he wanted to. And let me tell you, arguing with a demented person is futile. So is arguing with my dad…get it? My husband was the demented – oh never mind. But seriously, there is no reasoning with someone with dementia when the disease is in control.

Dad's mood swings created constant battles, though to some extent, I don't blame him. Imagine knowing you have a disease that affects your ability to think clearly, but also still wanting to be an autonomous adult and not knowing at any given moment if your brain is working properly. How do you know when you're right and when you're wrong if you *feel* like you're right? His perception of reality was different from ours, and trying to make him understand that was impossible. And when he'd tell us to go fuck ourselves, goddammit, we'd repeat in our heads "it's the disease, it's the disease, it's the disease." Even so, nine times out of ten, we'd end up cursing him right back.

On medication, his mood swings were less severe, but he was still constantly agitated whenever he thought we were blocking him. And if he didn't understand what we were trying to tell him, he'd get cranky and anxious. He'd get cranxious. For example, he couldn't follow directions unless they were broken down one step at a time. You couldn't say something like, "Dad, come around to the other side of the car and climb in the back seat and buckle up." He would get overwhelmed at the number of steps that were involved, curse at us, and stomp his feet. I think it scared him when he couldn't understand. We had to learn to only give him one step at a time. "Dad, come around to the other side of the car." Only after he'd done that could we tell him the next step of getting in the back seat. And again, we couldn't tell him to buckle up until he was already seated. We had to relearn how to communicate in ways that he understood.

We also started to learn the art of redirecting. Much like dealing with a petulant two-year-old, if you can distract them when a fit is coming on, you can often bypass or at least lessen the length of the tantrum. With my dad, music was the best way. Any time he got too agitated, we'd ask him to sing along with us, and that would usually calm him down. So would taking him for a walk on the train tracks – though in bad weather, that wasn't always an option.

But any time you had to redirect him, it usually meant that you had to stop whatever it was that you were trying to do in order to get him involved in a new activity. There were very few activities that would occupy him safely without supervision, so keeping him calm and happy and still maintaining any life of your own was impossible. Something simple like taking him for a swim was fraught with peril. He'd forget he needed to put on a swimsuit, so he'd strip down right in front of us and walk out to our pool, buns and penis flapping in the breeze. And if you were planning on swimming, too, there wasn't time to run to the bedroom to get changed yourself because in the minute and a half it took you, he would have already managed to jump into the pool with his $4000 hearing aids still in and his watch still on.

At Dr. Manning's suggestion, we enrolled Dad in adult day care. It was a lifesaver. A few days a week, we'd take my father to the Jefferson Area Board for Aging's adult-care center, which is a program to keep adults with dementia and other disabilities safe and entertained and give caregivers a break to go to work, run errands, or just get a little downtime. They pair up with a preschool next door so that there are intergenerational activities to keep everyone stimulated. They play games, do crafts, play music, and have a meal.

On Dad's first day, he called us about an hour after we dropped him off and said he was ready to come home. By his third day, he was hooked. Even on days when they were closed, he'd get up early to get ready because he was eager to go (which then meant, unfortunately, that we'd have to disappoint him by explaining that they weren't open that day). Who knew that a man who had hated games before the dementia would find them so thoroughly entertaining after it had taken hold? But it gave us a little room to breathe and put less pressure on us to keep him occupied throughout the day.

Our lives became a game of problem solving. We learned to redirect. We learned to communicate to him differently. We learned that every time we solved one problem, another would pop up. Each time he would stage down again, the old rules would have to be thrown out and we'd have to start again. Having Dr. Manning guiding us through was invaluable. Before we moved up, Dad had gotten lost in our woods, so she suggested marking a clear path so he could always find his way out. When Dad started forgetting which meds he'd taken, or if he'd taken them at all, she suggested putting them in a locked safe so that he couldn't access them without our help. When he tried to drive the tractor, she suggested a safe place to hide the keys. When we fought about him always wanting to be taken to the dump, she suggested set days. It was Dr. Manning who suggested creating a set schedule for watching Dad so that we all got some downtime. When he started getting up in the middle of the night and showering and dressing and fixing himself breakfast (by microwaving oatmeal for thirty minutes, thus waking us up with the smell of smoke – ack!), she suggested putting an alarm on the bedroom door to wake Mom up so she could talk him into going back to bed. When we were at our wit's end trying to keep him occupied, she suggested we take him to adult day care. She counseled us as a family as we fought to keep our own sanity and love for each other. She suggested that we take a day once a week to just do something fun as a family – we bowled, we flew kites, we went hiking, we sought out swimming holes in the mountains, we played on playgrounds, we had family dinners out, we looked for ways to feel some joy and to remind us of why we were all together. She helped us navigate around dozens of landmines just waiting to destroy us.

And when it was clear that we were just not going to be able to keep him safe and happy at home, Dr. Manning helped us give ourselves the permission we needed to start looking for a dementia care facility.

Chapter 4

Choosing a Dementia Care Facility

As it became clear that, even with three of us caring for him, we could no longer keep him safe, my mother and I began the hunt for a suitable dementia care facility. There are no words for what a depressing process this is. The conflicted emotions caregivers experience when making this decision cannot be overemphasized. I know that I, personally, felt an immense amount of guilt for several reasons. First, considering what a tight-knit family we were, I thought that it was my responsibility to care for him, and foisting him off onto someone else felt wrong. I felt guilty that we were clearly not meeting his needs. He was bored and agitated and angry that we were blocking him from doing what he felt compelled to do moment by moment. I consider myself a loving and caring person, and generally competent. I had volunteered for a camp for kids with special health needs and for hospice for years, and yet I was unable to give my father the appropriate care he deserved. I felt like a privileged white woman shirking my duties. I was so worn out, and I was tired of battling my dad at every turn. He had been my best friend and I was beginning to resent him. I was tired of not wanting to be around him and not feeling appreciated for having uprooted my life to move in and take care of him. I was tired of putting my life and my marriage essentially on hold without having any idea how long it would continue. I felt guilty for wanting to address my own needs. Sneaking around and looking at facilities without his knowledge also felt very underhanded. It felt like a betrayal. At the same time, it was important to recognize that we were failing to make my father happy because we were ill equipped to handle his busy-ness. We couldn't keep him entertained and out of trouble. He wasn't happy. We weren't happy. Something had to give.

Touring dementia care facilities, is a ~~special form of hell~~ bit surreal. The staff put on their very best face, but they can't cover the smell that assaults you when you enter the ward: that mixture of dirty diapers, overcooked food, cleaning supplies, mental decay, and confusion. It clings to your skin and memory, turns your stomach. It's hard to envision putting someone you love into a "home" that smells like this, knowing they'll never be able to escape it. We were lucky because my parents had purchased long-term care insurance about ten years before, so we were able to look only at the best facilities in town. I can't even imagine how bad the ones we didn't look at were. Generally, I remember the places we looked at being very cramped and dim, with residents parked in lounge chairs around TV sets. The brochures glowed about all of the programs they offered to keep residents occupied and happy, but we rarely encountered any of them actually taking place when we visited.

So, before I talk about how we actually made a decision about where and when to move him in, I'd like to offer some tips for choosing the right facility for your loved one, as well as some tips to any companies out there planning to build or adapt new dementia care facilities.

When someone you love is diagnosed with dementia, your world gets turned upside down. Navigating your new life as a caregiver can be tricky, and one of the hardest decisions is whether or not to put your loved one in a dementia care facility. First, when they're diagnosed, let them know you're going to see them through this, that you will stick around no matter how rough it gets, that you love them and will laugh with them and cry with them as needed, that you will do your utmost to get them the best care possible.

Do not make promises that you will never put them in a dementia care facility. If you have to renege on that promise later, there will be no end to your guilt. You may very well be in a situation where keeping your loved one at home is best for both them and for you (remember, your life counts, too). But there are also instances where keeping them safe at home just isn't a possibility. When my husband and I moved in with my parents to help Mom care for Dad, we were barely able to keep up. Even with three of us on shifts watching him, he was able to get into trouble. He was young, fit, and mobile – basically the world's most capable four-year-old – and we were afraid he was going to hurt himself or us accidentally. We needed a place where he would be safe.

I do not recommend visiting facilities with your loved one who has dementia. It will only scare them, because, let's be honest, even the nicest places aren't somewhere any of us *want* to end up. You can explore those possibilities on your own or with a friend or family member. Having someone along with you when the time comes to visit dementia units helps you talk things over and crystallize your feelings about each one. Take notes. And don't wait until the last minute to start looking. There are often long wait lists to get into dementia care facilities – particularly for men. It's better to get on a list early and turn it down if you're not ready to place them there than to be scrambling and desperate. Consider visiting places you like a second time – this time, unannounced. How things are working when they're expecting you may not be the same as when they aren't anticipating showing things in their best light. Aim for a mealtime as that seems to be a good indicator of how residents are treated. Are they sitting there not eating or being fed? Are they wandering around not eating? If they are, is the staff yelling at them to sit down, or are they using creative ways to redirect them? Does the food look edible? Is there a nutritionist on staff? My dad gained a *ton* of weight when he first moved in, in part because his meds made him thirsty and they'd give him juice instead of water. Because his disease affected his appestat (the part of the brain that tells you when you're full), he would eat and eat and eat, so they'd feed and feed and feed. If you put the food in front of him, he'd gobble it up. They didn't seem to realize that just because he snarfed it down didn't mean he was really hungry for more. For Dad, eating was just something pleasant to *do*.

Watch how the staff interacts with residents closely. Some people were made to do the job of working with those with dementia, others, not so much. Are there staff members sitting around reading the paper and ignoring the residents? Does the staff help each other problem solve? If a CNA is struggling to get a resident out of a chair, does someone come to his or her aid? If a staff member is unable to get a resident to do something, do they keep repeating the same thing louder and louder or say things like, "Don't you remember? We talked about this yesterday?" There are, sadly, some people who just really don't get it. They don't understand the concept of redirecting or soothing. They are frustrated when the residents don't remember that you told them the same thing six times already. The staff that are really great are the ones who can laugh it off that it's the eightieth time they've had to say something, or who try to figure out what's agitating a resident and soothe them. The ones who can make the crankypants residents laugh are geniuses. I commend their badassery.

Depending on the way your loved one's dementia has progressed, they may do better with smaller spaces, or they may need room to roam. Some people with dementia need to pace, so finding a space with both room to move inside and a safe place to wander outside is key. My dad's place had a large, open common room with lounge chairs, regular chairs, and tables with puzzles and activities, a dining room, and a couple TVs, as well as a music room and a sunroom. Outside, there was a fenced-in yard with sidewalks. The busier residents could do laps both inside and out, which helped with their agitation. Other dementia patients may need smaller, more confined spaces to feel safe and not get "lost." If you've been living with them at all, you'll know which seems better suited for your loved one. Having a couple different rooms for activities helps break up the day, especially for more agitated residents.

Other small details that will aid in your loved one's comfort: large name plates or "memory boxes" by their doors are helpful in getting them to identify a room as their own. We put a sign on my father's door with "Nick's Room" and a train on it. We also put photos and items that meant something to my dad in the memory box next to his door. It both helped him find his room, and let other people know a little bit about him, reminding them that he had been a fully functioning person once upon a time. If the facility doesn't have that option, consider just making a sign for the door to help your loved one identify their room. Another detail is multiple bathrooms near the common area. Ideally, there will be more than just a bathroom in the private or semiprivate room in case of bathroom emergencies.

Make sure the majority of the residents aren't wandering around in their pajamas. If they are, inquire about how often they're getting bathed and changed. When we first moved my dad in, we had an issue because he wanted to shower daily – it was an important part of his routine – and they only bathed the residents twice a week. We were able to work out a system of them getting him up early to bathe each day so he was happy – especially because he was still able to do most of the work himself – but it took some convincing the staff. When they figured out ~~how large a fit he could pitch~~ how agitated he got when he couldn't start the day with a shower, they became much more receptive to the idea.

Ask about what activities are provided. Is there a calendar of activities that gets sent to families so that you'll know when good times to visit might be (either to avoid the activity or fill in with some entertainment between activities, or even so you can come participate with your loved one in the activities being offered)? When you visit, is the activity listed on the calendar actually happening at the time listed? Is there any kind of regular music program? There have been several documentaries that have come out showing just how helpful music can be in making someone with dementia happy and more communicative. With my dad, even when he could barely speak anymore, he could still sing songs with us, and I felt like he was more alert if he'd been listening to music.

Does the facility restrain residents? I have mixed feelings about this one. Ideally, no, you don't want residents restrained to a bed or a chair. Restraints don't make for happy people, no matter their condition. But there are times that I wished it were an option. My dad fell out of bed several times and bruised himself up nicely. Bedrails are considered to be a form of restraint, and because his facility was restraint-free, it meant that we couldn't do anything other than put down some mats on the floor next to his bed in case he fell out again. Similarly, other residents had taken falls and had broken arms and hips because they got out of their beds or wheelchairs, not realizing they weren't able to walk anymore. It's one of those questions that doesn't always have a good answer. Do we keep them free and "independent" and risk them hurting themselves, or do we confine them and risk them being unhappy? You lose either way.

What are the long-term care options? This is a big one. If the resident becomes harder to physically manage, will they have to be moved to another facility like a skilled nursing center? What happens if the resident becomes violent? What happens if they get injured? Will someone accompany them to the hospital should an emergency arise (appallingly, the answer is usually "no")?

What are the costs? Most places will not only charge you for the bed and the meals, but also for anything bathroom related, such as adult diapers, wipes, soap, toilet paper, etc. They'll charge you for laundry. If you're local, it's not that big a deal because you can provide those things yourself – though hauling laundry home and back each time is a pain – but if you're not nearby, you should know that you'll need to factor in those costs. Prices for facilities range from about $3500 to $8000 a month. One of the smartest things my parents ever did was to get long-term care insurance when they each turned fifty. My dad's facility was almost $7000 a month, and their insurance covered most of that amount. But then he lived longer than the coverage lasted, so for a few months before he died, my mom had to pay that amount herself. Let's be honest, not knowing how much longer you'll have to do that is panic-inducing.

And lastly, is the facility you're considering somewhere you will be okay visiting your loved one? If not, then it's not the right place for them. If you hate being there, don't put them there. Even if you're sure you've picked a good place, you need to visit often and randomly. Your loved one can no longer advocate for him or herself, so you'll need to constantly monitor them and make sure they're being cared for properly. Your job does not end once they're in a dementia care facility.

Because my dad loved to be outside, finding a place that had ample room for him to roam safely outdoors was vital. My dad's facility did a relatively decent job, but a few things were lacking. A couple things to consider for any landscape architects out there who will be designing outdoor spaces for the hundreds of facilities that will no doubt be built over the coming years to address the needs of the aging population of baby boomers:

Make the walkways *wide*. Like, wide enough for three people to walk side-by-side. Since my dad couldn't walk very well on his own towards the end, it sometimes required a person on each side to steady him and keep him moving forward. And even when that wasn't so much the case, we liked to be able to hold his hands on each side as we strolled. And, obviously, keep the path as flat as possible.

Put bumper guards along the edges of the sidewalks so that those with wheelchairs or walkers don't accidentally steer themselves over the edge and into the plants.

Don't plant bushes or trees with poisonous berries. Residents with dementia don't know that they shouldn't pick things off of the foliage and pop it into their mouths. Think of planting things that wouldn't be harmful if ingested by a confused resident. At my dad's place, there's a lovely raised bed that they regularly changed the plantings in, but I sometimes wished they'd plant herbs and lettuce and other edibles for safety reasons.

Offer multiple benches along the path, some covered, some open. There was a nice gazebo at my dad's place that had three benches. It was lovely for sitting and enjoying the breezes passing through (the ones that were not emanating from my father's bowels, that is), and listening to birds, squirrels, and a nearby creek. It was a good place to just sit and be – away from the smells and sounds of other residents. When choosing the benches, think in terms of ones that don't require cushions, or if cushions are required, please, for heaven's sake, choose the kind that are wrapped in plastic so they don't get soaked if it rains, thus soaking the tushes of anyone unfortunate enough to sit before checking for dampness (i.e. pretty much all the residents).

Check for poison ivy. Frequently. Zealously. Please. We spotted it repeatedly at my dad's place and worried someone would get into it.

Make sure the fences are sufficiently tall so that the more spry residents can't climb it too easily. The day after we moved my dad in, he did just that – hopped the six-foot wrought-iron fence with the spikes on top. Perhaps consider very large trampolines on the outside of the fence to bounce them back in (now *there's* a mental image).

Put bird feeders outside of windows. The residents loved to watch for birds and squirrels at the feeders when they were in the sunroom. It brought cheer and life into the space.

All of that now out of the way, let's get back to my family's decision about where and when to move Dad. After touring several places, we finally settled on two places – one because we knew and liked the activities director and because the smell wasn't too bad, and the other because the layout was much larger and included a fenced-in back yard with walkways for my dad to roam – and put my father on the waiting list for each, knowing that, as they told us when we toured, it could be quite a while before an opening came up for a male resident. We were okay with that, because we didn't think my dad was quite far enough along to be ready for a place like that. Less than a week later, one of the two places called to say they had availability for a semi-private room with another male resident. Now go back and reread the sentence before that. We didn't think he was ready. Which gave us an agonizing choice: put him in while he was still so aware and likely to be very upset with the move, or wait, knowing that there was a very real possibility that it could be quite some time before something else opened up and we could be past the point where we really *needed* to place him. After talking it over with his therapist, who offered that it might actually be better to move him now because he was still capable of adapting to a new surrounding without it being too confusing, we decided to go ahead and take the spot.

We struggled with how to tell him, and finally decided to do it at his weekly therapy appointment. When we told Dad that he was going to have to live in a dementia unit, he said that that was just fine and that he was looking forward to it because we'd told him about all of the activities they had for him to do each day. We framed it that it would be like living in the adult day care center that he loved. He was surprisingly calm and unemotional about it. We proceeded to order his bed, look for furniture for his new room, etc., with him tagging merrily along to offer his opinion. We had been so nervous while secretly visiting the local dementia units to find the right one for him, and figuring out when we should make the move, etc., and we were so relieved that he seemed to be taking it so well.

Then we went to a store to look at bedspreads, and Dad pointed to one he liked and I said, "That looks good, but we need to find one for a twin size." He said, "But we have a queen bed." I explained that there wouldn't be room in his new space for a queen-size bed. It was then that he realized we would not be moving into the facility with him. He said, "You mean Mom won't be sleeping next to me anymore?" Then he started bawling. And so did I. I had never felt so cruel in all of my life. We stood in the aisle of the store hugging and crying, surrounded by linoleum and loud, cheerful bedspreads. My dad was gulping in air while he cried like a little child, and he was so raw and vulnerable and my heart felt like it was trying to flee my chest to enter his, to wrap him in all the love he was no longer capable of knowing we had for him.

After a few minutes when his crying didn't subside, my mom and I decided I should take Dad outside and she would stay and purchase the bedspread. As we got into the car, he continued to sob. Mom returned to the car and the weeping had not abated in the slightest. We needed to run to the grocery store, so my mom went into the store while I stayed with my crying father. He told me, "I just can't stop crying," so I asked him to sing me his favorite song. Within twenty seconds, he was happily singing songs with me. In bed that night as I cried myself to sleep, I wished the same thing would work for me.

Chapter 5

The Move

We moved my dad into the semi-private room on a Sunday. While Dad was at adult day care, Mom, Sebastian and I moved Dad's belongings into his side of the room. We hung familiar art on the walls, made sure there were coloring books handy, got a TV and a stereo set up, stocked the bathroom with his toiletries, put his clothes away and made his new twin bed. We met his roommate, a nice man who I'll call George (please note that I will be changing the names of the other residents and staff, as well, to protect their privacy). George was pleasant and didn't seem too out of it yet, so we hoped he would be a good fit for Dad. Because it was a Sunday, they were short-staffed, and it seemed weird that we were allowed to wander in and set everything up without anyone batting an eyelash or asking who the hell we were or if we needed any help.

Then Sebastian brought Dad over and we showed him around the facility. I remember being so nervous that I felt sick, but Dad was sweet and cheerful and kept saying, "Thank you, this is so nice" as we showed him where everything was. He was so utterly gracious about it. There were no activities going on because it was a Sunday and the afternoon activity leader hadn't arrived yet, so most of the residents were lined up in recliners in front of the TV, which just had the menu screen for a movie on (not even the actual movie). Not wanting to abandon him with nothing to do – especially after we'd told him the main reason we were moving him there was so that he could be constantly entertained – we strolled around the patio in the back, then sat down at a table and started coloring in coloring books. When lunchtime rolled around, we took him to the dining room where he commandeered a chair that had apparently been another resident's. But it was easier at that point to redirect the other resident, so that chair became *his* chair from then on. We sat and watched him eat and chatted with the couple CNAs who were passing out food, making sure they knew about his food preferences (such as they were at this point – he'd always hated seafood, but, along with his appestat no longer telling him that he was full so that he started packing on the pounds, his brain apparently no longer cared what flavors were in his mouth because he happily ate anything they put in front of him, including fish). The male CNA, who I'll call Mike, said he'd be sure that Dad got changed into PJs and settled in for the night properly. So we left and went to lunch ourselves.

I remember sitting at lunch and fighting back tears. I was racked with guilt and I was positive that we'd made the wrong decision after seeing that they had no activities happening and couldn't even be bothered to restart the movie instead of leaving the menu screen up. I could barely eat. But we'd made the choice and resolved to give it time.

The next day, we visited again. One of the activities people, who we'll call Maria, was playing bingo with the residents in the sunroom. We wandered up to Dad and all of the residents pounced on us, wanting to know who we were and what we were doing. It was, honestly, a little overwhelming, but knowing how I would want other family members to treat my dad, I did my best to repeatedly answer the same question over and over while trying to give my dad the attention he needed. He was sweaty and agitated, and angry that they hadn't let him shower that morning. We took him to the head nurse and she explained that the residents were only bathed twice a week. Twice. A week. Really?! For $7000 a month, you can't give them a daily shower? That's how Dad had started his day for the last sixty years, and now he was expected to just stop? We tried negotiating, but they said it wasn't possible because of staffing issues. When he started to get really angry, we worked out a compromise that they would wake him up a half hour before they woke everyone else up so that they could let him bathe, since he required very little supervision at that point. With that resolved, we returned to the activities room and got him settled in playing games and he was quite happy. After spending the morning with him, we left for lunch, feeling better about our decision.

About twenty minutes into our lunch, we got a call from the facility that he had escaped. Dad had wandered outside and climbed the six-foot wrought-iron fence with spikes on top that surrounded the walking path behind the facility. A fence *I* couldn't have climbed. Luckily, Mike noticed him through the window and hollered to some of the kitchen staff that were taking a smoke break to grab him. As he landed on the other side of the fence, my dad laughed, quite pleased with himself. Following the call to us from the worried staff, we raced back to see him. When I asked him what he'd been doing, he looked at me as though it should have been obvious and said, "I was trying to escape!" Yeah, we'd worked that one out on our own, Dad. So we asked if he was unhappy here and he said, "No, it's great!" with total sincerity. He just wanted to see if he could do it. We explained that if he did it again, they might kick him out, which I think sobered him up a little bit and he swore he wouldn't do it again. But just in case, we spent the majority of the following days hanging out with him in the facility in hopes that it would help him settle in. He did not try it again, and I think he really did just want to see if he *could* do it. The old coot.

But he was not done proving that he could escape in other ways. The facility was secured with a keypad with a four-digit code to enter or exit. Dad hung out at the keypad trying to figure out what the code might be. One afternoon, he proudly announced that he knew the code: 4501. He had even written it down on a piece of paper and was keeping it in his wallet. He demonstrated that it worked, which baffled the staff, because as far as anyone knew, the code was 4848. My father had somehow figured out a default code that no one knew existed. Maintenance fixed that glitch quickly. A couple days later, Dad announced that he again knew the code, this time giving them 4848, though he had not opted to use it to leave. No one could figure out how he knew it. The man couldn't figure out how to put on matching shoes, but he had turned into a damn code breaker! We should have sent him back into the military. World peace would have resulted. Sorry about not doing that, everyone, 20/20 hindsight and all that. Anyway, they, of course, changed the code again, and in the following weeks, he spent hours by the door staring at the keypad and trying different codes. As a result, the staff regularly changed the codes until his dementia progressed to the point where that desire left him.

The other time he escaped was a result of his age. Because he was younger than most of the residents, and still very mobile, he really just looked like a family member visiting a resident. One afternoon, a family was moving a new resident in, so Dad politely held the door open for them and wandered outside and down the street. Luckily, someone found him and brought him back before he could get hurt. Admittedly, it was not funny at the time and it caused us great anxiety, but looking back now, I kind of find all of his escape attempts hilarious. At the very least, he kept the staff on their toes and made them earn their keep.

The only other major hiccup we experienced early on after we moved Dad into the dementia care unit was that, one morning, apparently feeling as though his beard or mustache, which he had had roughly forty years and without which my mom and I had never seen him, was too long, he got up from a half-eaten breakfast and went to his bathroom and used his roommate's electric razor to remove all of his facial hair. When I came to visit, I didn't recognize him; such a strange feeling to not know my own father. It was jarring and a shock to the system and when I realized that the fat, clean-shaven man was my dad, I turned around and left the room to cry before he saw me. It was weird enough that he'd gained all that weight and looked like Santa (or jolly old Saint Nick, as it were), but then to have never seen him without full facial hair at the same time that we were losing so much of his personality – he was unrecognizable and it was heartbreaking. After he compulsively shaved a couple more times, the staff finally figured out that they needed to hide the razor where Dad couldn't get to it but where George could.

As a side note, twice in later years, staff at the facility took it upon themselves to shave off his beard or turn it into a goatee without asking permission. To anyone reading this who works with dementia patients, *please* do not change the hairstyle or facial hair of a resident without the family's permission. It is extremely distressing to arrive and find your loved one altered physically. I know it sounds minor, but when you've been slowly losing everything you know about him, having one more thing altering who you know him to be is too much. We dealt with enough changes with him becoming less and less like the person we knew. We didn't need it manifested physically. We dealt with the weight changes. We dealt with the vacant expressions. We dealt with his new body odor. Those were outside of our control and we accepted them and did our best not to be so bothered by them. But the things that made him look like *him* in any small way were so important to us. And, if he'd had the beard for the last forty years, don't you think it might confuse him when he looks in the mirror? So please, don't ever do anything to change a resident's appearance.

Before long, a private room opened up, and we opted to move him into it so that he would no longer have access to a roommate's personal belongings. The good news following his move was that we were free to just interact with him without the pressure of having to keep him safe and entertained. We were able to enjoy him and the fighting stopped. While he was still agitated much of the time, he was starting to mellow a little now that we weren't always "blocking" him. But as time progressed, so did the disease. He was less and less capable of getting my name right, though he would still light up when I came to see him. He still loved giving me hugs and kisses and singing with me. He was also speaking less, and normally you couldn't get more than "exactly right" or "yup" out of him. We still took him out to lunch to his favorite bagel shop, Bodo's, or for ice cream. We also took him to his weekly therapy sessions and to doctor and dentist appointments. We went for walks with him around the neighborhood for a while. But his world started to shrink.

PART II

Chapter 6

Thoughts From Afar

A word about the remainder of this book: A few months after we got Dad settled in in the dementia care facility, my husband and I moved to Raleigh to open a business. I returned home every month for a visit, but I obviously had less contact with my dad. During the time that we were living in Charlottesville, I did no writing or painting about any of this, but once I had some distance, I was able to start doing both. The remainder of this book will be the random thoughts I collected as our journey through dementia progressed. You'll be able to see my thoughts as the weekly highs and lows hit us, without the benefit of hindsight in the first part of this memoir. I have chosen, instead, to let you follow the journey as we experienced it, without any major editing.

***

Awkward Moments:

That awkward moment when your demented father looks at you and says, "I miss having sex with your mom. I wish I could still get an erection."

That awkward moment when you try to help your dad take off his coat and he proceeds to strip down naked and you have to restrain him from walking out into the common room *starkers*.

That awkward moment when you walk into the bathroom to find your father peeing on the floor.

That awkward moment when your dad walks up behind a stranger in a restaurant and kisses her on the head. Followed by that grateful moment when, after you apologize and explain that he has dementia, that stranger smiles and says, "Don't worry, I'm always up for a snuggle." Followed again by that grateful moment when the stranger leaves and her two little girls cheerfully smile at your dad and say goodbye.

That awkward moment when you're sitting on a bench seat at Bodo's with your dad and feel the seat rumbling. You know he has either just cut an enormous fart or crapped his pants. Either way, it's time to go. Followed by that awkward moment when you give him a hug goodbye after bringing him home and realize there is pee dripping down his pants and his shoes and it's probably on you now, too. Followed by that awkward moment when you walk outside and realize there is an entire trail of pee for about one hundred yards from outside through the front door, and you have to tell the staff so that they can clean it up.

After we put my dad into the dementia care unit, which I will call OLOP, I wrote his eulogy. I have tweaked it several times since then. I have no idea why I didn't wait until he died to write it. Maybe it's a way of preparing myself. Perhaps I won't want to face it when the time comes and so it's better to write it now. Maybe it's just a way of wallowing in my own sadness. My mom and I have talked about writing Dad's obituary soon so that we don't have to do it when he dies and we're a wreck, but so far, we haven't sat down to do it. What the eulogy has become is a long list of the things I already miss and will miss about him. I think I may have started to write it as a way to remind myself of the old him, the stuff that made me love him so fiercely. So much of that seems to be getting lost these days and is getting substituted by the current reality of who he is. Of course, the current reality shifts on a daily basis. We are constantly lowering our expectations, so that what we considered a bad day a year ago would be considered a good day now. But I know that I struggle, when I think of my dad, to think of him as he was before the dementia. Which, I suppose, is why, when I hear an old recording of him from his radio show or a home movie, I'm flattened. It's like being dropped in cold water and my heart seizes up and I'm unable to breathe. People tell me that, eventually, I'll go back to remembering him as he used to be, but I have to admit that I'm not convinced. I've already forgotten so much of the real him already. When I get sad and miss him, it's not even because I'm thinking of what we've lost. When an image of him pops in my head, it's the current, overweight, vacant-expressioned father that I see. I hope desperately that that will change when this is all over. But I know that when I think of my friends who have died, if I saw them in the hospital before they died, that's the image that most often comes to mind. I think of them sick more than I think of them well, because the sick part has gotten so tied into who I knew them to be. I suppose that's less true for how I think of my grandparents, so maybe there's hope about my dad.

***

My uncle called to check on me. He had called Dad to chat and Dad had told him that I had died a day or two before. When I asked Dad why he had said that, he replied, "Well, didn't you?"

***

The staff from the dementia unit called yesterday to let us know that Dad had kicked another resident in the stomach, then taken the lounge chair and swung it to try to finish knocking her down. Several weeks ago, he'd found another resident in his bed, and he'd grabbed her by the ankles and yanked her out of his bed and onto the floor. My dad has gotten violent. It hurts to think that the staff in the dementia unit where he is now never knew him before the disease. To them, this is who he is (though they try to reassure us to the contrary). This is not my father.

***

Mom took Dad to lunch at Bodo's, and the song "Don't Know Much About History" was playing. Out of nowhere, my dad said, "I got a B." We often find ourselves struggling to figure out what Dad's referring to, but it usually does pertain to the situation at hand in some convoluted way. Searching for context, she realized he must be referring to the song, and he had gotten a B in one of the subjects mentioned. She said, "What did you get a B in?" He replied, "In my bonnet."

***

Mom and Dad called me for my birthday and sang the happy birthday song. Dad got my name right. Best birthday present ever.

***

Usually, I didn't visit on Tuesdays before I left to head back to Raleigh because I had to leave while the residents were out on a "scenic bus ride," so I would either have to get up super early or leave later and risk being late for work. But on this particular Tuesday, I was adopting a kitten from the Charlottesville SPCA and had to wait until they were open before I could pick him up to drive him home to Raleigh, so I decided to visit Dad while I waited. I was waiting for him when the bus returned, and he saw me through the window and started blowing kisses at me and waving. He got off of the bus and came right to me to give me a big hug and kiss and then we went inside and started coloring in his coloring books. I was chattering to him about the new kitten and told him about our plans to possibly call him Testicles (pronounced Testicleez, like Sophocles) because he was a uni-baller (he was born with only one testicle), and Dad started laughing. Then he asked, "Are we going to Bodo's today?" My heart stopped. He hadn't asked me a question in about two years, and I was shocked that he knew that I usually took him to Bodo's when I visited. I told him that Mom would take him the next day and he said, "Okay, so you're getting a kitten?" I said yes, and then he asked me a series of questions about the kitten. I could barely breathe for the forty-five or so seconds that we talked like that, and then, just as suddenly, it was over and he was back to only saying, "Yup." For the rest of my life, I will never have a more beautiful forty-five seconds.

***

Whenever I feel like I need to start distancing myself from my dad to make it hurt less, something will happen that, to me, seems to be a sign to not let go. I was down in Florida attending a celebration of life for a friend who had died from lymphoma, and as I was leaving the event, guests for a wedding party were arriving. Among them, I saw a couple from the dementia support group we'd gone to in Virginia for a while. Neither of us could believe we were meeting there, of all places. The same week, my mom found her wedding ring that had been missing for a couple years. Are they really signs? I don't know. But I choose to take them to mean that it's not time to give up on him.

***

The staff let us know that they've found Dad sitting on the floor beside his bed several nights, so they think he may be rolling out. They are a restraint-free facility, so they won't put bars on the bed but have put a mat on the floor to hopefully keep him from getting hurt.

***

Sebastian and I were sitting outside with Dad on a lovely fall day, and I was snuggled up against my dad, who kept leaning over to give me kisses on my head like he did when I was little. Then I looked up and noticed that his finger was so far up his nose he was touching brain. I said, "You digging for gold up there?" He said, "Yup," then extracted his finger and immediately put it in his mouth.

***

New Year's Eve day, I stopped at the dementia unit to see Dad. The staff had gathered everyone into the music room and put New Year's hats and tiaras on everyone, and we were all singing along to songs. I was standing behind Dad, who was seated, rubbing his back and singing, and they started to play "Auld Lang Syne," and for some reason, the thought that this might be my last year with him, and the lyrics "should old acquaintance be forgot" combined and I just lost it. I ran out of the room bawling. Several of the staff saw me from across the main room and came over and wrapped me in love. One of them was crying, too, and said that she'd lost both of her parents this last year. I couldn't even imagine that. There are times when we get so angry with the staff for slacking off, but the fact remains that many of them do a great job caring for my dad so that it takes much of the burden off of us. And the love they showed me that day was epic.

***

The staff found my dad sweating profusely on the floor at two a.m. They called an ambulance and then my mom and said Dad was on his way to the hospital. Nobody was accompanying him. This was his second trip to the ER since moving in. The first was for swelling in his face and neck that turned out to be an allergic reaction to one of his meds. This time, they diagnosed him with pneumonia (though the staff at OLOP thinks what they witnessed was a cardiac episode that had resolved by the time he got to the hospital). He stayed in the hospital all day and overnight, with Mom staying on the sofa in his room to help keep him occupied and not wandering. When they couldn't get him to close his mouth around the thermometer, they took his temperature rectally. In the ER, when he couldn't give them a urine sample, they catheterized him. He did not like either of these procedures, of course, for good reason. Mom was in such shock and was so groggy that she said, after the fact, that she was having a hard time advocating for him. It got better once he was admitted and was being observed in a regular hospital room. He was thrilled when he got back to familiarity of the dementia care unit and he gave the staff big hugs and kisses.

When I came up to visit later that week, Mom and I sat down and had a talk about what constituted "life saving measures" in light of the fact that he had a do-not-resuscitate order. At what point should we stop the doctors from proceeding with treatment? Then we sat down with the head nurse at his facility for the same talk. We decided that, unless he needed something that would not require admitting him (like stitches or a cast), that he should not be sent to the hospital. We also discussed the wide array of medication and supplements he was on, and about scaling some of the supplements back. This is one of the hardest parts about being a caretaker: deciding, essentially, the best way for your loved one to die. Think about when you have to make the decision about putting your pet down. You obviously can't do that with a person, but it feels like the same decision in a way. Do you keep him on blood pressure meds to prevent a stroke so that he lives longer? What is the point of helping him live longer if he's going to continue to deteriorate? Is a stroke a worse way to die than pneumonia from aspirating his food? What is going to keep him the most comfortable? How do you help him maintain some dignity before he dies? When is treatment about quality of life and when is it about prolonging life? And when is the right time to say, "Don't treat the allergic reaction that could kill him?" How do we know when it's no longer appropriate to do that kind of thing? He can still talk, though it doesn't usually make sense and it's brief; he still laughs; he's definitely still mobile, though he limps and his feet and ankles have edema; and he's in diapers. If I know my father from his pre-dementia days, the diapers would be a deal breaker. But while he's still able to laugh and to walk, it doesn't seem right to not treat him for most things that could happen. Obviously, anything requiring surgery is out – except, what if he falls and breaks a hip? Would that kind of surgery be appropriate? And, selfishly, I'm terrified of the thought of him having a stroke or heart attack and dying before I can drive the four hours to get there. The thought of him dying without me being there makes my stomach turn.

***

I walked into Dad's room to visit him and said, "Hi, Poppa Bear!" Growing up, that was one of the many things I called him. He smiled and stood up to give me a hug. Mom and I started getting him dressed to go out for lunch, and he said, "Poppa Bear," a couple of times and chuckled. He did it again in the car, and again at lunch. From now on when I visit, I will call him that.

***

Lately, Dad does not seem to know my name, but he'll look at me and say, "Bodo's." I suppose, since I always take him to Bodo's when I visit, that constitutes some level of recognition. Why this intense need to be known? The head nurse, who I'll call Becky, was teasing him that she was going to "whup" him if he tried one more time to go outside in the rain, and he laughed and said, "Oh, Becky," and gave her a hug. When she told me this, I was thrilled and jealous. I wonder if he would know me any better if I saw him more frequently than twice at the end of each month? I wonder if he has any concept of just how much I love him, even though I'm not there to say it every day?

***

We have a struggle finding shoes to fit Dad. His feet have swollen and he can't get his shoes on and off easily. We switched from laced sneakers to Velcro sneakers, but he'd just shove his feet in and the tongue would end up in the toes of the shoes and he'd squish down and walk with his heels on the back of the shoes. He started walking really tenderly, and we realized it was because of the shoes. We bought several pairs of loafers, which had a similar problem with him walking on the backs but without there being a tongue to get shoved forward. He's started getting confused about where to use the bathroom, and several times he's pooped and peed on his shoes beside the bed, which is disgusting and difficult to clean up. Finally, out of desperation, we bought a pair of slip-on crocs that seem to work: wide enough for his swollen feet, easy to slip on, without much of a back to the shoes, somewhat supportive of his foot, safe to walk in, and easy to clean. We considered flip-flops, but decided they were likely to fall off or make him trip. He still shuffles when he walks, but does not appear to be in pain. We also have the challenge of his weight gain constantly necessitating buying new clothing that is easy to get on and off. Buttons become harder and harder to work, belts miss loops and are sometimes left unbuckled, shirts that slip over the head are hard to navigate. I can see why people kind of give up and let dementia patients live in pajamas. Like many of the other residents, when Dad doesn't know what to do, he gives himself something to do by taking clothing off or putting some on. We often arrive to find him wearing three shirts, unbuttoned pants, and only one shoe or two shoes that don't match. Then he'll be sitting there sweating, with all the layers on him in the summer, or freezing because he's taken a fleece off and is wandering around outside in a T-shirt in the winter. We've asked the staff to lock his closet to limit this, but they always seem to forget.

***

When you change Dad's diaper or his clothes, he gets confused about what he's supposed to be doing. You'll get him to take one arm out of the sleeve and then he'll immediately put it right back in instead of taking the next arm out. It becomes a bit of a wrestling match. If you insist too hard that he stop whatever he's doing, he says quite cheerfully, "Fuck you," and it almost sounds like he's saying, "Thank you." We have figured out, though, that if you get him to sing while you're helping him change, things sometimes go more smoothly. We've also realized that "fuck you" really means, "I'm frustrated or confused."

***

A couple weeks ago, I woke up in the middle of the night with a panic attack. I took some meds and eventually went back to sleep, but the whole next day, I felt anxious and like I was on the verge of another one. I wasn't anxious about anything in particular; I just had this sense of fear coursing through me. I found out later that Dad had choked on his food and Becky had had to do the Heimlich maneuver to save him. Was I picking up on his distress somehow? Is that even possible? I honestly don't know. Since then, he has been evaluated by a speech therapist who recommended that we cut up his food into smaller pieces and attempt to slow down his near inhalation of food. When we take him to Bodo's now, we tear the bagel up into small pieces and smear cream cheese on them, meting them out one by one like you would for a child. I worried that he would be frustrated and cranky about it, given how quickly he normally shoved food into his face and how much he hated being "blocked," but he patiently waits for each piece and takes a sip of his drink in between. Sometimes he smiles and gives me a cream-cheesy kiss.

***

Dad has taken to peeing in random places. It started with him going outside to the bushes whenever the urge to pee struck him. The awesome staff laughed it off and said he was just a man marking his territory, and did their best to assure the family of a new resident who were very concerned by the sight. He has lately progressed to peeing on the carpet next to his bed, though. Why the facility has carpet in the first place, given how many accidents residents have is beyond me. It's the lay-it-down-and-stick-it-on type, so it provides no cushion. So they have to have a cleaning crew come in several times a week to shampoo and dry his carpet. The smell in his room is awful, and I feel terrible for whatever new resident gets his room someday. Whenever I walk into the room, I have a moment where I have to suppress my gag reflex. I hate touching anything in there, and it's hard not to want to avoid touching him, even. I never thought I would wear gloves to touch my dad, but sometimes, it does come to that. Between the bathroom ickiness and the chronic nose picking, it's gross. Most of the time, though, I fight against my germaphobic self and hold his hand loyally. Then wash thoroughly and use about eight gallons of disinfectant when I leave.

***

I was reading someone's blog recently who has a parent with dementia, and the parent is still in the earlier stages, where they're very aware that they're slipping. I remember how painful that time was for us – when my dad knew that he was having a harder time understanding the world around him, but still felt like a reasonably autonomous being. I remember how angry he would get at us for telling him he wasn't understanding something, and how he pushed and pushed to be heard and treated like a competent adult, even when he no longer was. It had to be absolutely terrifying for him. There are times when I know I can't trust my own brain, because I have a very strong history of depression, but I also generally trust that at some point, I'll come out of the depression and be able to trust my worldview again. To be slipping and slipping and getting more and more confused, and knowing that it's not going to get better, well, I'm not sure how people continue on. But, blessedly, they get to the point where they're no longer aware that they're not seeing the world as it is for the rest of us. They can trust that the people around them are looking out for them, like a child does. At some point, they forget that they've forgotten.

***

I walked into the dementia care facility the other day, and Dad was zoned out and standing in front of some of the lounge chairs. A CNA wanted him to move so she could reposition one of the chairs, and he wasn't really paying attention. She reached out and started clapping in his ear like he was a dog and yelling, "Move, Nick!" How hard would it have been to take his elbow and gently move him out of the way? She was new and didn't know that it was his daughter standing there watching her do this. I witnessed another CNA yelling at a resident, "Don't you remember, we talked about this yesterday!" Um, you're in a dementia care facility. No, by definition, the resident with dementia doesn't remember what you talked about yesterday. Needless to say, the staff got an earful from me that day. How do you train people properly to get them to treat the residents with the dignity and patience they deserve? How do you teach them the path of least resistance in getting a resident to do what is needed? So many of them do not seem to get the concept of gentle touch, or not giving too many options or directions, or singing with residents to make unpleasant tasks easier. Is it something you can teach, or will some people just never understand?

***

Mom's cell phone died. She emailed me in distress, worried that if the OLOP staff tried to call her in the middle of the night that she would miss it. I know she's worried about her upcoming trip abroad. We have agreed that neither of us will go on vacation at the same time that the other one is gone so that one of us can get home in an emergency. I think we're reaching the stage where we live in constant anticipation of the next emergency that could be his last.

***

I received the following email from Mom about the dermatology appointment she had to take Dad to to assess a rash that they think is scabies (though none of the other residents has it, so we're not sure how he would have gotten it): "He was pretty patient with the paperwork and small bit of waiting. And had poop in his diaper. And I managed to change it by myself. And he only said 'fuckyou' once while I was doing it. So that wasn't bad."

***

There's a woman in Dad's facility that everyone pretty much can't stand. She's managed to stay surprisingly snobby for someone with dementia. Dad loathes her. Becky reported the other day that Dad walked by behind the woman where she was sitting and he bopped her on the head, then kept walking merrily on his way.

***

Every moment that my dad is even vaguely present with us should be savored, but it's so hard to relax and enjoy the moment when you know that it will be gone again the next second. How do you embrace the present when it could be the last time he says your name, or returns a hug? The fear that it will be the last taints the moment. When I visit every month, I try so hard to hold onto each second, but every time I say goodbye, I'm terrified that it will be the last time, and so can't fully enjoy the visit, even if he is more "with it." Every encounter is tinged with sadness and longing. Every interaction is laced with the fear of what is to come. Every moment that it feels like he has returned to us just makes the next one more painful for what we have lost. His more competent moments are bittersweet.

***

I called Dad to wish him a happy Father's Day. The CNA who gave him the phone told him that his daughter was on the phone and kept trying to get him to say "hello." I assume she was holding the phone up to his ear. I kept talking to him and calling him Dad, Daddy, Poppa Bear, etc., and telling him my name repeatedly. I asked questions about his day, wished him a happy Father's Day, and told him I loved him. He was completely silent. I finally said, "Daddy, will you sing a song with me?" He

45

immediately burst into "Sing a song of sixpence, pocket full of rye." So we sang that together and I thanked him and told him I loved him and got nothing back but silence. I told him to hand the phone back to the CNA and I hung up and cried.

***

To the gentlemen who were at the table next to ours at Bodo's today, Christmas Eve:

Thank you for not being offended when, while trying to steer my reindeer-antlered dad into the tiny gap between the tables and into the seat next to yours, he turned his butt toward you and stopped cold. Thank you for not being offended when I practically climbed over you to try getting at him from a different angle to get him to sit down. Thank you for not being offended when I collapsed in a fit of hysterical giggles on the table after three solid minutes of my mom, my husband, and me trying everything we could think of, from tempting him with hugs and kisses, to pushing and pulling, to singing, to telling him jokes, to getting him to say the words "sit down." Thank you for not being offended when we gave up for a moment and just said, "Uh-oh, we're stuck," when he would move neither forward nor backward. And, when we finally did manage to get him to back up and sit in a different seat, thank you for saying, "You handled that quite well."

To my father:

Thank you for not realizing my worst fear in that moment by farting in those gentlemen's faces.

***

My parents always said they'd travel abroad when they were both retired and did not need to be around in case of emergency for their aging parents. My dad got dementia before that could happen, but my mom had three friends who were widows who all decided that they wanted to travel now, while they still could. So she joined them on a trip to France and then a trip to Russia the following year. While she was in Russia, I got a call from Becky saying Dad had emerged from his room with a bleeding, swollen lip and a scratched cheek. Their best guess was that he had fallen out of bed and cut his lip on the bed rail and gotten rug burn on his cheek. I called a friend who worked near OLOP and asked her to go take a picture for me so that I could see how bad it was. After icing it for awhile, he was doing okay, and by the time I was able to visit a week later, it was healing nicely. But it underscored for my mom and me that neither of us will be able to travel outside the U.S. while Dad is still alive because this kind of thing, and other possible emergencies, are occurring more frequently now. And certainly, both of us should not be travelling more than a few hours car ride from him at the same time. It's amazing how, even with other people in charge of caring for him full-time, how much he still affects our lives on a daily basis – particularly my mom's. Her weeks are still filled with making sure he has clothes that fit as his waistline expands and contracts, shoes that fit as his feet swell, that he's getting bathed and changed and mentally stimulated, that he's fed properly to control his weight and to avoid choking, that he has aprons to protect his clothes when he eats, that he has coloring books and crayons, that his meds are being balanced so that he's not agitated, and, most importantly, making sure he knows she's still there and loves him.

***

We received a call from Becky telling us that, while playing bingo, Dad had put one of the tiddlywink sized bingo pieces in his mouth and chewed it to bits. It took three staff members to get him to spit any of it out, and he may have swallowed a little. They don't think it'll harm him, but "he may have confetti poop for a day or two."

***

Visited my dad this afternoon and almost had to take an elderly woman DOWN. Okay, not really, but kind of. I've seen videos of people with dementia that kind of pair up in their facility and become a "couple." It even happened briefly with a man and woman who are in the facility with my dad. I always thought I'd be able to handle the situation with appropriate civility and understanding, knowing that it isn't really a threat to my home and family. But today I watched this new broad sitting next to my dad and patting his arm and looking at him kind of adoringly. She also stared at me, and stared at me, and stared at me, but that didn't really unnerve me since most of the residents do that (I'm young-ish and female and smile at everyone, so they're drawn to me and I'm used to it by now – plus, I'm devastatingly attractive, so who can blame them, right?!). Her staring kind of freaked Sebastian out, though. She was in a chair close to my dad and could reach him quite easily, and I was stuck a little ways away in another chair and, well, I felt…threatened. That's *my* job to pat his arm. That's *my mom's* job. Back off, old lady. I'm younger and quicker and not to be trifled with. Now, Dad was totally oblivious to all of this. I don't think he was really even aware that she was there, but still. Interestingly, apparently the woman's husband complained to the staff not long after she moved in when he saw my dad pat his wife on the head as he walked by (he does this to everybody). Here we are feeling threatened by his wife patting my dad's arm. Sigh. Now I want to meet her husband and pat him on his head and let him pat me on my arm and we can all agree that we're okay.

But if she does it again, she better sleep with one eye open.

***

You'll be pleased to know, dear reader, that my dad is not pregnant. Nor does he have uterine cancer or ovarian cysts. The OLOP staff called us late last night to say that his belly was swollen and hard and they were going to do an X-ray. Of course, I immediately looked up possible reasons online, and most sites listed those three causes as the most likely culprits. So, when they called this morning to say that the X-ray showed nothing and he's acting totally fine, we were very relieved. We don't need any little demented babies running around that place. If he *was* pregnant, I know exactly who the mother would be. That same lady I told you about who was patting his hand is still after all the gents in the joint, and when I sit with Dad she tries to kill me with just her thoughts. I think she might be training to be a Jedi master. The staff kept telling her that I was Nick's daughter, that he was married, that she was married, that Nick was not her husband, etc. She'd blink at them and then go back to glaring at me. And since he was in a hug-y and kissy mood with me, she was downright livid. So, in response, I tried to tickle her with just my thoughts. No dice. Oh well, I'm headed back to Raleigh today, so she can go back to just hating my mom. And we can go back to being relieved that Dad doesn't have a bun in the oven.

***

Bit of a rollercoaster here the last couple days. As mentioned before, my dad is not pregnant, which is great. The X-ray came back negative, so we all breathed a sigh of relief, and I went home. Then we got a call from Becky saying that he might have a hernia. So we scheduled a doctor's appointment for him the next day, then commenced turning apoplectic at the thought that he might have to have surgery. How the hell do you keep a relatively mobile patient with dementia from getting up and tearing stitches and generally hurting themselves? What effect will the anesthesia have on him? Will the dementia get worse? Are we hastening his death by putting his body through trauma? I have to go to New York for a wedding this weekend – what if he has surgery while I'm gone and something happens? Needless to say, I slept nada last night. Spent the morning reminding myself to breathe and pacing around the apartment. Then my mom called from the doctor's office, and the doctor said that while, yes, it is a hernia, it's not causing him pain (i.e., he doesn't flinch when she pushes it back in or moves his legs around), so we'll watch it but not do anything about it. So no surgery. Yaaaaay! It's been about five hours since the office visit and I'm just now starting to breathe normally again.

Making decisions for my father is tough, because he's not verbal and doesn't understand what's happening and can't explain to you what he's feeling or not feeling. And deciding what needs to be done for quality of life in a way that doesn't prolong or shorten his life isn't easy. I'm glad we got to dodge actually making a decision this time around, but it was a reminder of what the weight of his life feels like in our hands.

Having kind of a rough day over here, y'all. I was listening to a podcast of Mindy Kaling being interviewed on *Fresh Air* yesterday, and she talked about how her mom changed after her terminal-cancer diagnosis. Her mom was sick for a few months and then was gone, but in that time, she seemed like a different person. Several months after her mom's death, Mindy said that she's getting back to remembering who her mom was before the disease took hold. After this many years, I find that I have a hard time thinking of my dad as he was before the dementia. My idea of him has fundamentally altered, and I'm not sure that, after his death, time will return his old self to me. If I can't remember that stuff now, why would it come back after he's gone? I remember snippets, like isolated snapshots, of who he was, and why we were so close. I can remember, generally, what his qualities were, but the incidents that demonstrated those qualities? Not so much. I know he was funny, and a great listener, and my biggest supporter, but I can't tell you why. I'm afraid that, when this is all said and done, I won't get those back. I want true memories, not vague ideas. I want something concrete, and I'm terrified that all I'll be left with are these painful, specific memories, of how the disease has robbed me of him. I don't want to remember the tantrums in the grocery store or how he cried when he realized that my mom wouldn't be moving into the dementia care unit with him. I don't want to remember hugging him and pulling away to find that he's wet himself. I don't want to remember him staring at me with no recognition.

Perhaps when he dies and we have a memorial service, people will tell me stories that will trigger more solid memories for me of my dad before dementia. I really hope so.

***

Another panic attack last night. Got word today that Dad's gait was really odd and he wasn't being nearly as responsive as usual. They're running blood work and trying to get a urine sample. Any other day, he'd be peeing all the damn time in every place he could find. Today? Nope. Of course. There was talk of admitting him to the hospital for observation, but Mom reminded them that we wanted to avoid that if possible, and the staff and doctor agreed. Update: tests came back normal and he returned to his usual self by the end of the day.

***

A quick reminder to anyone with a loved one in a dementia care unit: Even though you're most likely paying more than you can afford for people to give your loved one top notch care, you need to be double-checking that it's actually happening. Even with my mom visiting Dad several times a week, things get overlooked. She assumes that the people who are paid to care for him are caring for him. Go figure. When I was home for Christmas, I noticed that his fingernails were long and really jagged where he'd bitten pieces off, so I filed them down (a disgusting job given all of the foods and bodily fluids that accumulate under this nails). His skin is really dry with all the cold weather, and my mom has provided multiple bottles of lotion for the staff to slather up his stomach and back because he gets really itchy. I *think* they've mostly been good about that, but no one has been trimming his nails on any kind of regular basis, and it definitely hasn't been done since I was there for Christmas last month. As a result, he has scratched himself raw and drawn blood. I teared up when he lifted his shirt to itch and I caught a glimpse of the bright red crosshatching marking up his stomach. Mom asked someone again a week ago to make sure that his nails got trimmed, and as of yesterday, it hadn't been done, so we did it ourselves again. We are paying obscene amounts of money, and are really disappointed that this basic care has not been provided. I ended up going in today to talk to the higher-ups and the nurse in charge about this and a couple other things, like making sure there's soap in the wall-mounted dispenser in his bathroom, and making sure there's always a staff member around the main living area to keep an eye on the residents who aren't participating in activities. They seem chronically understaffed.

For the most part, his care is good, but on several instances, we've basically had to shame them into basic things like changing him out of his pajamas in the morning and into regular clothes. We've had to write letters, hang signs in his room explaining the difference between pajamas and not-pajamas, and talk to staff members reminding them of our expectations, which I don't think are unreasonable. We're not asking them to wait on him hand and foot (although, honestly, for what we pay, they should be), but they are always reactive to the issues that pop up (and usually only because we've had to speak up about it) and very rarely proactive in preventing the issues in the first place. You would think Dad was their first dementia patient and they'd never seen these things before.

So, if you have opted not to keep your loved one at home, check on them. Regularly – even if the staff really seem to care. And by "regularly," I mean often and at random times of day so that they don't start to expect you at certain times only. If your loved one doesn't live nearby, find someone you trust who can check on them. Regularly. If you can't do that, consider moving them closer. Even the best facilities can slack off if family members aren't there to advocate for the residents.

All of that being said, I am pleased to report that he was having a good day yesterday, and was very smiley and happy to sing along, and tolerated his manicure admirably. He was definitely out of it Sunday and today, but I'm awfully glad for the giggles we got out of him on Monday. And I'm a sucker for his hugs and kisses. Those moments when he genuinely laughs are like rainbows stitching up my heart.

Deciding which vitamins and medication to keep someone with dementia on can be tough. For example, we recently had to decide whether or not to give my dad the pneumococcal vaccine. I'm not going to tell you what we decided, because, honestly, I don't need anyone telling me we were wrong, but I wanted to give you some insight into what goes into the decision-making process.

With frontotemporal dementia, the thing that's most likely to kill my dad is pneumonia. As his brain winds down, so does his ability to swallow, which means he'll aspirate food. It'll cause an infection, and he'll get pneumonia and die. So, considering whether or not to give a vaccine that could possibly prevent that isn't something to take lightly – especially in our society, which places such value on length of life regardless of quality of life. We're taught to do everything we can to help our loved ones to live as long as possible. It's deeply ingrained in us, so every time my mom and I stop to think about whether a medication is right for him, we feel guilty if we choose an option that won't prolong his life. Our main reasoning behind each vitamin, medication, or other treatment that he continues to receive is that it prevents pain, not death. Because he's going to die, no matter what we do. But we don't want him to suffer if we can help it. Pneumonia, though, will cause some suffering. So, of course, we want to prevent that. The thing is, we really can't prevent it, because it's pretty much inevitable that, barring a heart attack or stroke, that's what will cause his death. So preventing it seems useless. And what if it makes it so that he gets it but less severely, goes through that pain, lives, and then has to do it all over again one or more times before the pneumonia wins and he dies? Let's say he doesn't get pneumonia this year, but he does next year. He'll be in much worse shape over the coming year as the dementia continues to progress, and if he were to die from pneumonia tomorrow, that might save him more pain. And knowing who my dad was before the dementia, I think he would not want to be like he is now and would want this all over. But how do you not give someone something that could save his life? And if he does get pneumonia with or without the vaccine, should we treat it at this point?

You see the circular thinking that happens here? The pros and cons kind of balance out. And we're guaranteed to feel guilt, no matter what. If we don't give him the vaccine, and he gets pneumonia and dies, I'll feel responsible. If we do give it to him and we have to watch him lose more and more of his dignity daily, and we extend his life longer than he would have wanted, we feel guilty. And even worse, finances do come into the decision – at least in part. Currently, my dad's long-term care insurance pays for most of his approximately $7000-per-month bill for the facility where he lives. That will run out soon, though, and my mom will have to take on that burden, which is scary. Her father lived to almost ninety and her mother lived to ninety-eight, so odds are that my mom has another at least twenty years to go and will need that money herself, which means that the burden will fall to my husband and me to take care of her if it runs out. The worst sentence you ever want to have to write is that you can't *afford* for your loved one to live much longer. It should never, ever, have to factor into your decision-making, and we mostly don't let it and we figure that we'll work it out down the road, but that fearful thought is floating around the back of our minds.

I'm doing my best to eliminate guilt through this process. I'm making the best decisions that I can possibly make to give him the care he deserves. But I think that it's inevitable that I'll feel at least a little guilty in the end, because we're forced to make very hard choices in interpreting what his wishes would be. Frankly put, it sucks.

***

Just finished up teaching a painting class that included an elderly couple who had been brought in as a surprise by their daughter. Watching the pair, I was pretty sure that the woman had some kind of early dementia, and every step I gave I had to go over and get her started and, in some instances, do the whole step for her. She just sort of sat there blankly for most of the class. But whenever her husband leaned over and whispered in her ear, she lit up like the Fourth of July and started to giggle. Then she'd reach over and start painting on his canvas instead of her own, and he just let her do it and made jokes about her taking over his life.

That's the way you do this whole dementia thing, friends. Have patience and make them laugh.

***

One of the tough things about having a parent diagnosed with dementia is the realization that, not only are you going to lose someone you love bit by bit, but you may inherit the disease and lose yourself bit by bit. It's a terrifying prospect. There are tests for some Alzheimer's genes, but currently no such test exists to see if you carry a gene for Dad's particular form of dementia. Luckily, there aren't strong hereditary links for frontotemporal dementia, so perhaps I'll at least be spared that particular dementia. Even for the kinds of dementia that you can test for, it doesn't guarantee that you'll develop the disease or when it would start; it just shows that it's a likely possibility. I can't decide if knowing it's going to happen is better or worse than not knowing. The fear is there either way, and I'm not one who can talk myself out of knowing it could happen. I suppose I would rather know, though, so that I can plan my life accordingly or maybe recognize the signs earlier if they come. I do live with a bit of dread, and every time I forget something or misplace something or have difficulty understanding something I'm reading, I panic for a moment, even though I'm only in my thirties. I do know that I have thought a lot about what we are going through and I know I do not want to put my friends and family through the same thing. If I get dementia in any form, I am going to do my damnedest to try to end things before they get bad. The trouble is, of course, how do you know when things are bad when you're the one with dementia? At a certain point, Dad stopped knowing that he didn't know. I know a lot of people reading this will find this offensive, and believe me, it's not something I take lightly. While I'm not religious, I do worry about what will be, essentially, suicide, and what that might do to my soul if I do, in fact, have one. When my dad was first diagnosed, I wrote him a letter saying to remember that we were all in this together and that he shouldn't do anything he thought of as heroic in trying to spare us the pain of what was likely to come as the disease progressed. While I'm grateful for every minute I've had with him, looking back, I don't know that that was good advice. He would be mortified at needing his diaper changed and not being able to recognize his friends and family. I'm horrified at the thought of losing him a second too early, but I also know how hard it has been to have him dying in pieces over the last few years. You're in a constant state of grieving with no closure possible until he has finally died. It's agony. It's emotionally, spiritually, and financially exhausting. And what is the point of living out the progression of the disease? To lose all dignity, exhaust everyone around you, and bring them pain – it just doesn't seem kind to myself or my family. But again, I'm torn at the thought of my dad. It would have been devastating to have lost him too early. It's devastating to have been going through this for this long. There is, obviously, no good answer. But I know that I don't want to be debased the way my father has been.

***

My mom called a couple days ago and, as always, my heart leapt onto a plane and de-boarded in my throat. We text and email pretty much daily, but she rarely calls. So when she does, I have a moment of panic and assume something awful has happened to my dad. Rarely is this actually true. When she called this time, she was visiting him and thought I'd like to chat with him, which generally goes like this:

Me: Hi, Poppa Bear!

Dad: …

Me: Daddy! Are you having a good day?

Dad: Yup.

Me: Excellent.

Dad: …

Mom: It's Emily on the phone. Can you say hi?

Dad: ...

And then Mom and I chat and he sits there either staring at her phone or off into space. Sometimes I break randomly into song and can get him to join in for a few words. Then we wrap it up and go on our merry ways.

This time, Mom said that Dad had had another choking incident sometime in the last week. The facility had not called to tell her, which they are supposed to do, so we're not sure what day exactly. But they had to do the Heimlich on him again. After the last time, they had a speech pathologist assess him and they were supposed to be cutting everything into small pieces at mealtime and only giving him a little at a time, so he couldn't shove everything on the plate into his mouth like he's that competitive-hot-dog-eating kid. I've sat in on several meals since then and some of the staff remember, some don't. So, no real surprise that it happened again. He didn't seem at all phased by it by the time I talked to him, so no real harm done, I guess.

What's hard for me, though, is the thought of him being scared or hurting in that moment. That thought kills me. If Dad is so confused normally, it's hard to know what goes on in his head when he suddenly can't breathe. Is he scared? Is it painful? Does he understand that, when the nurse wraps her arms around him and shoves her fists into his stomach, she's saving his life? The fact that I can't protect him from these experiences is awful. The fact that I can't protect him from the dementia in general is worse. It's hard to live with.

Mom called again today and said that, like normal, when she visited him today, he wasn't really present much, but she was holding his hand and chatting to him, and when she said it was time for her to leave, he held her hand tighter, like he didn't want her to go. Normally, he doesn't seem to care much either way these days, so that was unusual. He kept holding on and kissing her hand, which led us to speculate that something from the choking experience earlier in the week had affected him, which, truthfully, is not likely. It's more likely that she just got lucky and was there during a brief moment where the window opened and he could see her. Those moments are getting scarce.

All I can do is hope that my dad knows just how loved he is. And I'm hoping that someday I can put all the broken little pieces of my heart in a locket to wear around my neck.

***

Sebastian and I were shopping for some furniture for the new house and saw a penny sitting on top of a chair, and I just lost it. I started crying right there in the furniture store. One stupid lucky penny and

I'm a wreck. We decided to treat ourselves to ice cream, and someone at the ice cream stand here in Raleigh was wearing a Bodo's T-shirt from Dad's favorite bagel shop in Charlottesville. And then, on our way to another store after getting ice cream, we passed a store called Nick's Trains.

So there I am, a hot, fragile mess, trying to pull it together before going into the next store, and I stopped and thought about it. And what I decided was that, with all the horribleness that this week has contained, maybe the universe was actually trying to remind me of how lucky I am. I have these silly memories of putting out lucky pennies, and chowing down on the best bagels in the country, and train watching and flattening pennies on the track, and setting up model trains in the basement – all with my dad. And now I'm teary, but for good reasons.

Thanks for the bitch-slap, powers that be. I needed that.

***

A word to the wise: If your father is dying, it is best to not leave the house or watch TV or listen to the radio for the month of June. Avoid all malls, grocery stores, florists, restaurants, bars, and anywhere with a TV or radio. The Father's Day advertisements are *everywhere*, and they all tell me they know exactly what my dad wants this year. But let me tell you, he does not want the ultimate beer-making kit. He does not want a tie or a mug. He doesn't want a man-cave makeover in the basement. Nor does he have any interest in increasing his movie collection or getting tickets to see his favorite band. I already know what he wants. He wants to pick his nose when he's inclined, to eat the food off of his neighbor's plate at the table, to fart, poop, and pee wherever and whenever the urge presents itself, to wander at will around the dementia care facility, and to get and give hugs and kisses to anyone and everyone who smiles at him. So, until June twenty-first, I'm hiding in a hole I've dug under a rock hidden in a forest far, far away, and surrounded with sound-proofed walls and furry woodland creatures who give me wiggly-nosed kisses and don't mind when I do all the things my dad wants to do.

***

Lest you, dear reader, think that everything related to my dad is wailing and pulling at hair and gnashing of teeth, let me reassure you that we do, in fact, find things to laugh about along the way. For example, the other day, he was in a group activity, looking to all the world as though he were asleep. The activities person was playing word games with the residents, asking them for words that start with each letter. When she got to "j," my dad – eyes still closed – piped up with "justification!" The man can normally barely utter more than "yup," but he came up with a five syllable word that no one around him was likely to have been using beforehand for him to parrot. When we came in a couple days later to visit, the nurse said, "They're in the music room, doing meditation. Nick's meditating on justification." Yes.

Dad spends a lot of time with his eyes closed, though he's definitely awake. When I came in on Sunday to visit, he was sitting there with his finger wiggling in his ear. It went on for about ten minutes. My theory is that he was trying to scratch his itchy brain. It happens.

He also has a tendency, as mentioned before, to have very itchy skin, so it's a battle to keep him moisturized and his nails clipped so he doesn't compulsively scratch himself raw. He also likes to chew his fingernails down to the skin, then keep chewing, and then chew some more, and a little more after that. He's a big fan of meals that include fingernail with a side of skin. But who can blame him? Skin is delicious, apparently. Nails, too. Anyway, we've started giving him a teething ring and a couple other baby toys to occupy his hands and mouth and hopefully reduce the likelihood of him gnawing his way to the bone in his finger. He sits there, eyes still closed, playing with the toy for hours. And then Mom texted me a picture of him as she found him on one visit: a toy in each hand and a teething ring in his mouth. Whatever works.

***

The dementia care facility is redecorating the unit, and has repainted its walls. It needed it badly, but the color scheme they've replaced it with is, well, questionable. It's a combination of puce, yellow ochre, and teal. Shuffling past one of the brownish-green doors, one of the residents observed, "Ew. It looks like baby shit." Needless to say, I love that resident.

***

So, life kicked my heart in the crotch again yesterday. Then it gave it a paper cut and poured Mike's Hard Lemonade on it, which properly sterilized the wound with alcohol, but still hurt like a sumbitch.

The powers that be where my dad lives announced to my mom this week that, because he's staging down again, he's about at the point where they'll need to move him over to the skilled nursing wing. Whatthewhat? When we moved him in, there was no mention about having to totally disrupt and disorient him once he got to a certain point. We were under the impression that he could live out his remaining time where he was in order to make it as gentle and stress-free a process as possible. And we've seen other residents do that. Now, suddenly, we're being told otherwise. To make matters worse, the nursing wing is DE-PRESS-ING. Not that it's all sunshine and unicorn kisses on the dementia care side, but we're used to it – Dad can roam as he's able, the staff knows him, he (mostly) knows the staff, and it's now his home (and has been for almost five years). The nursing wing is dark, with narrow halls, and residents lined up in those halls staring forlornly at the wall across from them and moaning at anyone who goes past. The only activities we've seen are meals and a small TV with room for about five patients to watch. And what's even more messed up is that there are residents still in the dementia unit that are way further along in the disease progression, so I don't understand why they can stay but he can't.

So we spent part of yesterday visiting other nursing care facilities to see if they're all as depressing as the one they want to move him to (answer: no, there are others that are much more cheerful). But we also learned that skilled nursing centers may not be appropriate for him since he doesn't require any rehab and we won't be doing any life-prolonging measures so he won't need things like IVs. So now we're thinking we need to call hospice and ask their advice about what an appropriate facility for him might be. Then, our goal is to tell the higher-ups at his current residence that, if he is not allowed to stay in the dementia care facility, he will be taken elsewhere, and hopefully when they realize they'll lose that income, they'll allow him to remain in his current situation. So cross your fingers.

As if that whole adventure wasn't delightful enough for the day, we also went to the cemetery where my mom just bought a plot and a bench for putting Dad's (and, eventually, our) ashes when the time comes. It's a lovely spot in the cemetery below Monticello, Thomas Jefferson's home. It's right beneath a tree and has mountain views on either side. And two fawns were playing in the pasture near us. We also have some distant cousins and some family friends buried there, so we figure my dad can have a rollicking party when he arrives. Good company for eternity and all that. Hopefully there will be Scotch on hand for him. For some reason, the fact that it was a lovely spot and quite peaceful made me lose it. Or maybe I would have lost it anyway (this is assuming, of course, that I have ever had it). I'm not sure that I can articulate why. But I pictured myself sitting on that bench, staring at those mountains that have always brought me so much comfort and peace, and just aching with missing him. And I started aching in that moment, and did that really attractive thing where you do the shuddering-and-sucking-in-air gasps, trying not to cry. And then Mom said, "It's okay to cry," which is just the worst and best thing, because you do. Losing him while you haven't lost him is so damn brutal. Trying to get this stuff out of the way now, while it's less painful and there isn't a hurry, is probably a really good thing, except that it's still really freaking painful anyway. Sitting there designing the bench and figuring out what we want to say on it, and do we want a plaque for his military service, and do we want his full dates or just the years, and are there any little decorative things we want on it, and do we want vases for flowers, etc., was just too much and will always be too much.

So anyway, my heart feels a bit like it sat on the couch for twenty years and then went for a twenty mile run – stiff and sore and in serious need of a good soak in the tub and a large glass of bourbon.

***

We contacted hospice to see if they could give us any recommendations for places that were high quality and would allow my dad to die in place, but they aren't allowed to give us that kind of info. We talked with the staff where he is now to stress how much we don't want to move him, and, if they insist, we'll have to move him somewhere else because we can't stand their skilled nursing unit. We've checked out several places, and will check out more if necessary.

In the meantime, a friend suggested to my mom that if Dad were enrolled with hospice's services, he wouldn't have to move because then the OLOP staff would have the additional help they say they need. So we talked to his doctor who agreed he could be enrolled at this point, so the facility has arranged for an evaluation, which will happen tomorrow. My mom called me to tell me this yesterday, and for the most part, I'm fine with it. I'll do whatever possible to keep him where he is now so that he doesn't have to go through a move and all the confusion that would result.

But when I stop to really think about it, I'm not sure what to wish for. Do I want hospice to take him on, confirming that he is, in fact, likely to die within the next six months or so (their standard criteria for providing services)? Or do I want them to reject him because he's not that far along yet? I desperately want him to be able to stay in what is now his home, and part of me is just as desperately holding on and hoping he doesn't die any time soon, terrified of the day when I won't be able to give him a hug or see him smile. I lose my breath just thinking about it.

So for now, I guess all I can do is wait and see what hospice decides, and deal with it as it comes.

***

Hospice has agreed that it's time for my dad to be enrolled. I feel the need to explain what hospice is as there seems to be some confusion with friends. Having volunteered for them while I was in college and then later when I lived in Florida, I understand their services pretty well. Many people think that hospice is a facility where people go to die. While many hospice organizations do have such facilities, that is not the only thing they do. They can come to anywhere a person with a terminal illness lives to provide palliative care (i.e., non-life saving care) and respite for caregivers. Their doctors and nurses help manage patients' pain to ensure that their final months are as pain-free as possible. Staff and volunteers can help with bathing, or meal preparation, or taking patients out for some sun, or reading to a patient while a caregiver runs errands. They offer a huge array of services. In college, I visited patients and sang with them, or read to them in the hospice facility. In Florida, I did respite care in people's homes and then did what they called "eleventh hour care," which meant that I sat in nursing homes with patients who were in the process of actively dying but who didn't have family that could sit with them while they died. When I was a teenager, my parents actually volunteered with hospice and took the children of a patient out for some playtime, doing everything from walking the mall or going to a playground, to taking them out to eat, to taking them to meet our horses. What's the most amazing thing to me is that all of hospice's services are free of charge to the patient.

So anyway, Dad is now officially enrolled, and we're hoping the additional help they'll be providing will allow him to stay in his current home. They've already arranged for a wheelchair to be brought in because he's been slowing way down and having some trouble walking steadily. They're also going to take over bathing him, so that will take some pressure off of OLOP's staff. So things are looking up.

***

As Dad starts to wind down, my mom and I are trying to prepare for his actual death as best we can. This includes talking about the tough stuff like which cremation service to use, what kind of memorial service to have, where we want to inter or scatter his ashes, etc. We are slowly lining things up so that, when the time comes, we won't be overwhelmed. This is good, and is helping us emotionally prepare, though I am a little bit concerned that we'll have taken care of everything and we won't have anything to do to distract us when his death actually happens. When someone dies, historically, I go into "do" mode. I help plan the service, I clean out the person's closet, I contact the people who need to be contacted. It keeps me occupied and not wallowing in pain, helping me to cope and to allow the grief to come in a little bit at a time, not as an onslaught. But we've been grieving for so long in this instance, that that distancing by "doing" may not be necessary this time around.

As part of our preparations for my dad's death, we've purchased a grave site and ordered a bench where his ashes can be interred, and that has three other spaces for our own ashes someday. We have the option of having something short engraved on the bench. Since Dad will be, ahem, getting the most use out of the bench, it seems appropriate to choose something like lyrics from a jazz tune since Dad was a jazz musician. I've been going through my song books looking for options. Here are some of the lyrics I've rejected so far:

"I'm a glum one"

"I've got you under my skin"

"Don't you know, you fool, you never can win"

 "Doo wah doo wah doo wah"

"My heart does not stand still just hear it beat"

"I keep wishing I were somewhere else"

"When you are with me it's worse"

"I'm limp as a glove"

"My new lovers all seem so tame"

"Mental deficient you'll grade me"

"You've cooked my goose"

"I'm suing for damages"

***

This past weekend, I went home to visit my parents, and I've been processing everything over the last couple of days and gathering my thoughts on how to write about the visit. My dad's seventy-third birthday is tomorrow, but I won't be able to be there, so we decided to celebrate while I was visiting. He's past the point of fully understanding what it means to have a birthday, I think, and he certainly couldn't tell you what day it was or how old he was, but, seeing as how this is most likely his last birthday, given how far the dementia has progressed (just writing that, my throat catches), it was important to my mom and to me to acknowledge and celebrate it. We picked up balloons and a crown and an ice cream sundae and brought it to him. He'd open his mouth reeeeeeeeeally wide waaaaaaaaay before the spoon got anywhere near it, then drip half of it down his beard like a little kid (if little kids had beards, that is. That'd be creepy. So maybe not like a little kid. Maybe more like a three-toed sloth). It was quite cute.

I snuck in three visits over the three days I was home, and the first day was really lovely outside, so we wheeled him out in his brand new fancypants wheelchair to look at the changing leaves and enjoy the breezes. We did a couple laps around the fenced-in courtyard (while getting passed several times by two residents who were all giggly and up to no good, but who I adore because they're so stinkin' cute), and then we parked him looking out at the woods and creek behind the courtyard. We sang a little, and gave him lots of kisses, and then, for a moment, as I was pulling back from giving him a kiss, he looked at me. Right. At. Me. He didn't say anything, but I felt like he was present for just a second, and he *saw* me. The world kept spinning madly around us, but for just that second, we were still and together and that's all there was.

It's amazing how my view of what constitutes a good interaction has changed over the last few years. It used to be whether or not he could sit still long enough to look at photos or participate in an activity. Then it was how much we talked and sang. Then it was if he got my name right. Then it became whether or not I could get a belly laugh out of him. Then it was how many hugs I got. And now, a good visit comes down to him making eye contact for a second or two. And soon, it'll be if he's awake. And then there will be nothing.

It feels almost surreal that he's the same person I grew up with, because who he seems to be now is worlds away from who he seemed to be then. And now I'm grateful for *eye contact*. I say that and it seems absurd, and ridiculous, and heartbreaking. But still, I'm grateful. If he hadn't been so amazing a father, this wouldn't hurt so much. I'm lucky.

On Tuesday, I visited right before heading back to Raleigh. He was lined up with the other residents in his wheelchair with a blanket on him, watching *West Side Story*, so I pulled up a chair next to him and held his hand and sang along with the tunes. And then it came time for me to leave, and I went to give him a hug. And I realized, with him in the wheelchair full-time now, I'm never going to get a giantdaddybearhug again. I can lean over the chair from the side, and kind of get my arms around his shoulders, and he can reach a hand up to touch my back, but he can never wrap me in his arms again. And then I realized I didn't pay nearly enough attention to the last time he gave me a real hug on my last visit up. And I should have been holding on and savoring and burning it into my memory, but it's too late now. And I'm devastated. It makes the future where I don't have his physical self at all seem way too near. It makes me ache. No amount of preparation will make it okay. So we just keep looking for the tiny things that we still have and try to etch them into our memories so that they're not lost forever when he's gone.

***

Do you ever have those days when it seems like the universe is trying to tell you something? As a not particularly religious person, I don't know what to make of those times. For example, yesterday. After a particularly rough patch surrounding my feelings about my dad's birthday, I woke yesterday morning feeling much better. We're on vacation in Blowing Rock, NC, so I was all set for a day of exploring the local shops, drinking my favorite chai in all the land, taking lots of photos, soaking in the hot tub that overlooks the river below the cabin we're renting, and binge watching HGTV. Everything got off to a good start and we headed into town and started perusing the quaint little stores in Blowing Rock itself. In the first art gallery we went into, a song was playing that reminds me of my dad, so I got a little teary, but nothing major and I was able to brush it off and enjoy the art. Then, since I actually get a signal in town, I checked my email on my phone and got a message from a friend who was listening to my dad's CD. She wrote, "Listening to Nick play and reading his words on the CD insert. I am feeling thankful for this little piece of him sealed in time." So sweet of her to send me that. SO sweet. But having had it just follow the song I'd heard in the gallery, it got me a little teary again, though mostly in a good way. About thirty minutes later, Sebastian and I were in another store and someone had made a little sign reading, "I love you a bushel and a peck" which are lyrics from a song I sing with my dad every time I visit.

And that was the final straw. Constant reminders of him are too much right now. I lost it, standing in front of that little sign. Sobfest '15 commenced. Here I was, trying to step away from the things weighing on me for a couple days, allowing myself to be okay and not have a nonstop grief-fest, and it was like the universe was wagging its finger at me, saying, "Not so fast!"

But I can't imagine that I'm *supposed* to be sad all the time. Packing up those feelings for a few days is healthy, necessary. So what's the message I should be picking up? It's not like I'm in danger of forgetting my father. I wasn't in a phase where I needed comfort and reminders that he's still here.

Sometimes I wish I had a decoder ring that would tell me what I'm supposed to be learning when it seems like the world is smacking me upside the head with love and pain. If someone could get me one for Christmas, you'd be my new best friend. Kpleaseandthankyou.

*****

As hard as this has all been on me, I can only imagine what it's done to my mom. She's having to go through all of this without her best friend. That person she would have talked to about life's major events, happy or sad, was my dad. Now he *is* life's major event, and she can't exactly talk to him about it. She can talk to me, but I know that she sometimes has a hard time letting go of the role of protective mother and feels like she needs to be strong for me. This, of course, just adds to her burden. I'm thankful that we're as close as we are, because I know there are other people who have to go through this without even the benefit of a supportive child. And Mom and I have turned into a spectacular team in navigating through this dementia journey.

Someone once said to me that, as the spouse of someone with dementia, you have to put on a face for the world of the brave wife or husband, when you really just feel like collapsing most of the time. And part of you wants to move on with your life, but you're tethered to someone who has become almost a stranger. Your marriage is essentially over, but technically, it's not. So you're caught in this purgatory, simultaneously hoping for and dreading the day you'll be released from it.

It's hard to witness the effect this has had on my mom's social life, too. There are people who have disappeared from my parents' lives following his diagnosis. I'm not sure if it's the fact that he was so young and it made them face their own mortality earlier than they'd planned, or their fear of his sometimes strange behavior in the early phases. Maybe it's that they don't know how to "help" so they hide, not realizing that the best way to help is just to continue to offer friendship to my mom. The number of years over which this has stretched also kind of stretches people's patience and generosity, I think. I recognize that, especially now, it's hard to know how to support my mom when she's a widow who is not yet widowed. But the people who have pulled back have no idea that what they're doing is making things even harder on my mom. Their fear hurts her, because it makes her feel like she's losing her friends, her support network. It makes her feel like they don't really value her friendship. If someone had let her down before, who would she have talked to, seeking solace? My dad. That's no longer an option, and I'm doing my best to take his place, but I don't live there, so she can't come home at the end of the day and cry in my arms. She's already losing her best friend to dementia, so to not have other friends step up makes her feel alone, abandoned. Even now, when he's been enrolled with hospice – a time I would have thought would have had people coming out of the woodwork to offer words of comfort – friends continue to desert.

My dad was always the social organizer, the life of the party. I worried that my mom would become a hermit of sorts, but she's made an effort to reach out and has crafted her own social life. The reason she's been able to do this is because of the people who have stayed. Those people – the ones who have not shied away from the ugliness of the disease or the awkwardness of interacting with my dad – those are the people who made her life bearable in the early phases. Those are the people who hold her up when it gets really hard. They're the people who don't wait for her to ask if they want to do something, but instead invite her over for dinner or out to a play, who don't treat her like a pariah who might give them dementia, those are the ones I respect. That takes courage. And loyalty. And compassion. A lot of her friends are at retirement age, so are traveling and aren't available. It's not their fault, but it's bad timing for her. So the ones that make an effort to see her when they are in town, even if only briefly, help substitute some of the love she's lost. The neighbors who have stepped in and welcomed her into their families are wonderful. The friends that organized trips to Europe together get gold stars. The ones that make plans and stick to them – understanding how awful it makes her feel when her plans get canceled at the last minute and she doesn't have a husband to go home and snuggle with – are bright shining rays of love.

It's a sad fact that misfortune shows you who your real friends are. And some people will totally disappoint you. But there are also people who step up and surprise you. People you didn't even know cared extend invitations, offer hugs, and just let you know they're here if you need them. They know they can't fix it or make the loneliness go away, but they keep sticking around, and jumping up and down and waving periodically to help you find your way back to them, and saying, "We're here when you want us to be here."

To the ones who stay, thank you. If you're recognizing that you're one of the ones who haven't, it's not too late. If you feel guilty that you let my dad down, make up for it by lifting my mom up.

If you don't know us and this doesn't pertain to you, stop and think about other situations in your life when you've chosen to face discomfort or fear to remain a good friend, or maybe the times you fell a little short. Please don't let shame about falling short stop you from starting again and making up for it. In the end, you'll be a lot happier avoiding the guilt you'll feel when someone dies and you had let them down in some way. I've learned that the hard way. Send a card. Make a call. Meet for coffee. Invite someone over for dinner. Drop cookies off at the house for no real reason. Rise. Stay. Be there. It's worth it and lifts someone when you have no idea how down they really are because they're busy putting on a brave face. Stay. Be there. Stay.

***

It's funny how grieving can sneak up on you. Most of the time, honestly, I'm pretty okay with where we are in my dad's dementia journey. I'd call it a "struggle," but really, we're past the point where there's anything to fight, so "journey" seems more appropriate. While I think of my dad every day, and certainly have moments where the enormity of where we are hits me, I manage to keep the tears and panic at bay a good portion of the time. But there are those times where the grief sneak attacks you. A couple days ago, I was talking to my mom, and she said that a man she knows from the gym asked to talk to her about the Memory Disorders Clinic at UVA because he knew we had taken my dad there for several years. Since we adore Dr. Manning, who was our counselor there, Mom was happy to share our experiences with him. When Mom sat down to talk to this man, she learned that he, like my dad, has frontotemporal dementia. As soon as she told me, I said, "Fuuuuuuuuuck." I don't even know this man, and I started tearing up. I was devastated for him. He's only in his sixties. Just like my dad. He has a daughter named Emily who is just about the age I was when my dad was diagnosed. Just like my dad. He has stopped driving after failing a diagnostic driving test. Just like my dad. He has been struggling at work and had to retire. Just like my dad. He was scared. Just like my dad.

When Mom told me about this, I was immediately brought back to the early stages of Dad's disease. I remember the terror of what the future would hold. When I look back at that time, it felt like the world was ending. My tears start flowing remembering how much emotional pain my dad was in. I grieve for how he felt and how I couldn't make it better for him, how I couldn't protect him. I grieve knowing that he has become exactly what he was most afraid of being. So when I learned about this man that Mom talked to who is somewhat newly diagnosed, it throws me back into that time, and I grieve for him and his family. I know at least some of what lies in store for them, and I wish I could protect them, too. As Dad's disease has progressed, and I have had to adjust to the new normal repeatedly, I start to forget where we've already been. Each new stage feels devastating. Now that he's nearing the end, it feels like this is the worst place to be. But remembering how it used to be, that feels equally like the worst place to be. In some ways, I'm grateful that we're no longer there. Don't get me wrong, I'd give anything to go back to the time early in the disease where he could still laugh at my jokes, or could dance with me, or share his love of music, or just give me a proud-papa look. But that time was also incredibly hard, because he was scared and angry and frustrated and cognizant of the fact that he was losing himself. He had so little control over his emotions and his actions, and he accidentally hurt us, too, sometimes. So while I'd love to have so many of those things back, he's in a better place now that he's beyond knowing what he's lost.

***

Last night was the second time since my dad was diagnosed with dementia that I truly got mad at him. It's not even remotely his fault, but I'm angry. So goddamn angry.

The first time, I was home alone with him one night during the year that Sebastian and I lived with my parents to help care for him. My mom and Sebastian were each out of town, so I was home taking care of him by myself. It was time for bed, so I sent Dad upstairs, thinking he could get himself to bed. Not long after he'd gone up, he came downstairs and knocked on my bedroom door and, in a very cranky voice, said he couldn't sleep because there was a light on making his bedroom too bright. I figured it was a light from the back porch, so I went to double check and saw that it was still on. I turned it off and sent him back upstairs again. A few minutes later, he came down again and irately told me that I hadn't solved the problem. I had to get up early the next day, and I was exhausted from having watched him on my own the last couple days, so I told him that the light was already off and he needed to just go to bed. And then he told me to fuck myself. My father, who had been my best friend, who had never cursed *at* me my entire life, told me to fuck myself. That's when I just lost it. I screamed at him. Just. Plain. Screamed. I told him I hated him. I came incredibly close to hitting him. I was so angry at how he'd upended my entire life and now he was telling me to fuck myself? I'd moved in to care for him, leaving behind my house and friends in Florida. I had no life in Virginia now that I lived with him because he constantly needed watching. I stormed upstairs, pretty much dragging him behind me to prove that the fucking light was fucking off fucking fuck fuck fuck. When we got to his bedroom, there was indeed a light still on and blazing through the window. At some point in the day, he had turned on a light from a different porch and his room was ridiculously bright and there was no way he could have slept like that. He wasn't crazy; he just didn't know how to turn it off again. I felt horrible. I had dismissed him. It was not his fault. The cursing wasn't even his fault. It was the disease. I haven't been truly mad at him since.

Last night, I got mad again. Really mad. Raging mad. And once again, it was not his fault. The facility has decided that he absolutely must be moved to the skilled nursing wing that we hate. We had enrolled him in hospice because someone had suggested that if the facility staff had extra help from hospice staff, he could stay put. So we did that. But apparently, that's not enough. They're "not licensed for full care." They're only licensed for assisted living. A small detail they neglected to tell us when they were selling us on the place. No one said he wouldn't be able to age and die in place. They kind of ambushed my mom at the care-plan meeting today with that little tidbit. She called me afterward, sobbing. So now we either have to move him to this dark, depressing, awful facility linked to where he is now, or go searching again for a different facility where visiting him won't be so terrible. And spend the money and the time to have him moved. And his long-term care insurance has run out, so it will all be out of pocket.

The thought of him being more disoriented and possibly scared and unable to tell us he's scared breaks my fucking heart. And I'm tired of my fucking heart being fucking broken. I'm tired of being a caretaker. I'm tired of being a parent to my parent. I'm tired of fighting to get him the care he deserves. I'm tired of having him not recognize me or what I'm going through. I'm tired of trying to choose the least awful option for him. I'm tired of walking the line between getting him great care and extending his life unnecessarily. I'm tired of caring. I'm tired of feeling like I've got an open wound that no one can see, and still having to put on a happy face at work and pretending like I'm not so utterly exhausted by grieving for the last almost seven years that I can barely think straight. I'm tired of watching him suck the joy out of my mom's life. I'm tired of having to watch her battle everyone around him just to keep him safe and whatever version of happy he can be.

I feel so horribly, horribly guilty for feeling like I just want this over. No more. We've been through enough. I know it's selfish, but right now, I don't even care. I know I'll regret feeling this way once he's really gone. I know I'll wish I had him back regardless of his condition. But I don't care right now. I just want this to go away so I can move on. I'm tired of one crisis after another.

I sat on the bathroom floor sobbing last night and wishing my dad would choke on some food and die. Or wishing a nurse would accidentally give him too many meds and his body would finally call it quits. I'm so fucking mad at him for putting us through this. I mean, I'm mad at the disease, but it's manifesting through him, and therefore he's the target of my wrath right now. I feel so guilty writing this, but I need to get it out of me. And I'm betting there are plenty of caretakers who've felt this way. So I'm just going to say it.

I'm angry at him for getting this disease. I'm mad at him for putting us through this, even while I know he would never in a million years have wanted this to happen to any of us. I'm just so fucking mad. So mad. So. Mad.

***

Feeling useless in Raleigh following the announcement that Dad would absolutely have to be moved, I drove up to see him and my mom on Sunday, and we spent Monday figuring out where to put him. Distressingly, there were very few options for someone at his level of disease. This is worrisome in light of all the baby boomers that will be needing services like this over the next twenty years. The system will be completely overwhelmed. But that's beside the point.

Because we had almost no options, we decided we'd take another look at the skilled nursing center at Dad's current facility. Most of their rooms are semi-private, but as luck (for us, at least) would have it, a one-hundred-eight-year-old resident passed away Monday morning, making a private room available. Now, my dad doesn't need a private room at this point – having a roommate most likely wouldn't bother him one bit – but for our sake, we wanted one. I can't imagine, if he gets sick and is actively dying and we're trying to have alone time with him, what it would be like to have another resident and their family coming in and out of the room. Not the ideal situation, though plenty of people do it.

We took the official tour with the admissions administrator/social worker who, it seemed to me, somewhat disingenuously cooed at and kissed the residents who were in the hall as we walked past. We're still not crazy about the place, but it seems to be our only real option, and we'll be watching like hawks, so we opted to take the available room. When we went to visit my dad in his current unit, Becky, who we really like, came over, looking worried and a little expectant. She had apparently clocked out but was waiting for us to come down because she'd heard that we were touring the nursing side. When we told her we were going to take the room, she exhaled and started crying. She was so relieved and it was obvious how much she has been dreading the thought of not seeing him daily. There are several staff members who work in both units, so there will be people who already know how to care for him without us having to train them, and in his more lucid moments, it may bring him comfort to see familiar faces. And I know Becky will be keeping an eye out for him, too.

While I'm not thrilled that he has to move, I know we've chosen the best option currently available for him. That's all we can do.

***

About two weeks later now, the big move has happened. My mom and a friend moved my dad's belongings over to the skilled nursing unit on Monday, and were supposed to be moving him over, too, but there was some kind of staffing glitch. So Mom moved Dad over on Tuesday instead. I didn't hear much from Mom about it, so I assumed everything was okay. Checked in a few times, and she was doing alright. The next day, she texted a picture of him lined up in the hallway, just like we'd feared they would do to him and just like they promised they wouldn't. But some of the staff from the dementia care unit did make an effort to get over to see him on their breaks. So there's that. I texted with her last night because she's caught in the blizzard hitting the East Coast and I wanted to make sure she was okay. She was not. As she put it, it was killing her to not be there with him. We had lost power and I was trying to preserve my cell-phone battery's charge, so I couldn't call her, but I spoke to her today now that our power is back on. She said he seems really sad. He wouldn't engage with her at all. No response to the normal cues that make him chuckle or even give a one word answer. No singing along to his favorite tunes. Even the activities director, who knows him from the dementia wing, said he seemed sad, so we know it wasn't just Mom projecting her emotions onto him. Exactly what we were afraid of happening. I hate the thought of his final days/months being sad ones. I hope he's not scared. He doesn't deserve this. I feel like we're failing him even though we checked out every option and I know we chose the best one.

Really, it's not us who are failing him, but the powers that be at the facility who insisted we move him. The system is failing us. There are no words for how furious I am at them for doing this to him and to us. I hate how far away I am because I can't be there to hug my mom and give her comfort. Being stuck at home in a blizzard just leads to too much time to think and worry. This blizzard is exceptionally bad timing, because Mom being able to visit Dad would bring both of them a little solace right now. And I can hear the pain in my mother's voice. She's been so incredibly strong through all of this, but I can feel her heart breaking. I want to wrap her up in love and protect her from it, but I can't. We have to face it. And we will. But it sure ain't fun.

***

On Sunday last week, I drove up to VA to visit my parents. It was my first time seeing my dad since he had been moved to the new facility. He had declined significantly since my visit a few weeks before. We sat with him for a while and got the activities person to file his fingernails, then fed him his dinner. On Monday evening, we headed back over a little before dinner so we could be there to help feed him again. The staff seemed ill-equipped for feeding as many residents as they had. In fact, about forty-five minutes after he was supposed to be served dinner, they still had not come to get him or three of the other residents, and since he wasn't in his wheelchair and we weren't able to lift him, we couldn't wheel him down to the dining room ourselves. I finally had to go ask the staff to come get him and the other three residents. To be fair, they were dealing with a new resident who was demanding a lot of extra attention, so I was trying to be sympathetic. But it was so indicative of how they run things in that facility. We even heard them refer to the residents that required assistance with eating as "feeders." They said it right in front of the residents and in front of us. So rude.

One of my dad's childhood friends, Charlie, and his wife, Jan, drove down from Ohio that night. We took them over on Tuesday for a visit. When we arrived, Dad was getting physical/occupational therapy to see if he could stand up to make changing him easier, so we left and got lunch and came back. As we were walking in, Dad's doctor was coming out and stopped us to talk. Dad had developed bedsores from shearing (basically, he was sliding down in his wheelchair and it was stretching the skin and causing sores), so they were going to start having him lie down for an hour or two after meals to take the pressure off of his bottom. They were also going to order a new wheelchair that would allow them to shift the tilt so he wasn't putting pressure on one spot for too long.

He was lying down when we went to his room. He wasn't very alert, but he did open his eyes some and look at us, and Charlie (who plays piano, sings, and is a choir director) and I sang songs to Dad. Mom and Jan joined in, too, so Dad got quite the concert. He did not join in, though. We also reminisced about their childhood so my dad could hear it. The next morning, Charlie and Jan went over a little before Mom and I because they needed to get back on the road. When they got there, he was in bed again, and there was rock music playing on his radio. Not knowing that Dad's CD player hadn't worked for the last three years or so (Dad had been stacking CDs in like old forty-five records and had broken it), he popped Dad's own CD in and, miraculously, it played. We were surprised but delighted. After Charlie and Jan said goodbye, Mom and I headed to the dining room for a care-planning meeting with the staff. The meeting went okay. We managed to be firm but gracious about his care needing to improve and about how hard a transition it had been for my dad. He had been so sad after we moved him.

After the meeting, I went into Dad's room to say goodbye before I drove back to Raleigh. I whispered in his ear that I was going but that I would see him soon. He opened his eyes and looked directly into mine and started moving his mouth like he was trying to say something. I had the overwhelming feeling that he was saying goodbye. I can't tell you why I thought that, but I did. I started bawling in the hallway when I hugged my mom goodbye, but I didn't say anything to her about it, because I thought maybe I was wrong and was projecting or something. A couple hours into my drive south, I had a full-on panic attack, so I pulled over to call Sebastian and told him that I thought Dad had said goodbye to me. He tried to reassure me that it probably wasn't that and that I likely had a while to go, but that maybe I should keep a bag packed in case I had to go up again suddenly. I finally calmed down and continued driving home, white-knuckling it the whole way because we were having a serious thunderstorm and I could barely see. It normally takes about three and a half to four hours to get home, but between stopping for the panic attack and having to drive thirty-five miles an hour in a seventy-mile-an-hour zone, it took me closer to five hours.

As I pulled into the driveway, Sebastian came out and said that I shouldn't bother unloading the car. Mom had called about five minutes before and said that Dad had suddenly started having trouble breathing and hospice thought I should come back right away. So I threw some more clothes in a bag and Sebastian drove me back up. I got to his room around ten o'clock that night, and we began our vigil. The first night, Becky, Dad's favorite nurse, was actually on duty in his wing, which was wonderful. He was relatively restful, though his breathing was too fast and his limbs were spasming a little from lack of oxygen. They had started him on oxygen and morphine. They were also concerned that his hernia had worsened and might be causing some pain, and they needed to roll him into new positions periodically to avoid the bedsores worsening and causing still more pain. That night, my mom and I "slept" in wheelchairs in his room. There wasn't enough room for all three of us to stay, so Sebastian headed back to Mom's house and slept there. Over the course of the night, Dad's breathing grew more labored, and the spasming intensified. We tried to play some other CDs to soothe him now that the CD player seemed to be working, but no CD other than his own would play. Of course.

The next morning, Sebastian came to say goodbye because he had to go back to Raleigh to take care of the cats and our business. He's not generally good with death, so I was worried he would avoid saying goodbye to Dad, but he actually asked for a couple minutes alone with him. He's had a rough relationship with his own father, and in marrying me, he felt like he was finally getting the father he's always wanted. He adored my dad. Watching him say goodbye was tough, but I'm proud of him for doing it, because he won't have that regret later.

The hospice staff came back and talked to us about what was happening. I'm familiar with the dying process from my days volunteering with hospice. All but one of the patients I'd sat with while they were dying had been pretty peaceful, and the one that wasn't had had cancer. But Dad wasn't even close to peaceful. The hospice nurse increased his morphine to every two hours with a prn (i.e., as needed) dose in between if he seemed to still be in pain. She also prescribed liquid Ativan every four hours to help with the muscle spasms and said we could sprinkle the pill form under his tongue and add a tiny bit of water until the liquid version arrived. By the evening, he had gotten worse and was clearly in pain. The OLOP nurse on the evening shift was totally incompetent. She didn't know how to use a pulse oximeter (that little thing they put on your finger to monitor your blood oxygen saturation), she gave him a Tylenol suppository without taking his temperature, and she didn't seem to understand the concept of a prn dose. We had been tracking what time he was getting his morphine doses, and she was consistently late giving them and refused to give a prn dose in between even though she, herself, noted how much pain he seemed to be in. She said she didn't want to lose her license. He was dying, but she was afraid she might kill him? She also had not yet gotten the liquid Ativan, so she crushed a pill up into a small cup of water and tried pouring it into his mouth, which made him choke. So she stopped trying to pour it in and he never got a full dose. She wouldn't listen to us about anything and finally said, "Hospice should really be here doing this, not me." I said that I agreed and that I would call them but that I didn't have their phone number. She said, "I've got it in my pocket. They told me to call if there were any issues." I stared at her, dumbfounded. I got the number from her and called hospice at about ten o'clock that night. While we waited for the hospice nurse to arrive, I tried doing guided meditation with him, rubbing his chest and saying things like, "Breathe love in and let it replace the pain. It's working its way into your arms, and now into your hands. Feel your muscles relax. Feel all the love you put out into the world coming back to you." I don't know if he understood anything I was saying or if it was just the soothing tone of my voice, but it did seem to help a little while I was doing it. But as soon as I would stop, his pain would amplify again.

The hospice nurse arrived around eleven-thirty and called his doctor and they upped his medications, but by that point, we were playing catch-up. We were never able to get on top of the pain for him. The night-shift nurse was on top of things – she set herself a timer to remind her when it was time to give him his next dose and was never late, but we just never caught up to his runaway pain. That night, the hospice people arranged for the staff to bring in a couple recliners for us to sleep in so we didn't have to have another night in the wheelchairs. Mom and I took shifts, singing and soothing him as best we could, but even when it was our turn to sleep, there wasn't a lot of actual sleeping going on because every time my dad moaned, we would both jump up and check on him. I'm not a religious person, but I was begging whatever powers might be out there to stop this pain. He didn't deserve this.

Several of the staff from the dementia care wing came by to see him, which was incredibly sweet and touching. But, almost to a person, they'd poke him and shout that they were there to see him. I understand that they're used to dealing with residents who are hard of hearing, but Dad wasn't. It was frustrating that they were jabbing him and shaking his arm to make him acknowledge they were there. Hold his hand gently for a moment to let him quietly know he's loved. It doesn't matter if he knows it's you specifically. If he's resting, don't disturb him. If he's in pain, don't make it worse. Just a little side note in case you, dear reader, ever visit someone in their final hours.

By about six o'clock in the morning on Friday, the death rattle had started. We kept telling my dad that it was okay to let go; that we were going to take care of each other so he didn't need to worry about us; that he had done well in his life and his work was over. And every time we said it, he'd moan a little louder. We both knew that a lot of people pass when their loved ones leave the room, but he was in such pain we didn't want to leave him. Our hospice team arrived again a little later in the morning, this time with the social worker there, too. At a little after eleven o'clock, a hospice aide came in and offered to give him a warm sponge bath, and we agreed that that would be good. We each kissed my dad and told him that if he needed to go while we were out of the room, it was okay. We talked a little while in the hallway with the social worker, and then walked over to the dementia care facility to see the new furniture they'd gotten. In the ten to fifteen minutes that we were gone, Dad died.

I don't blame the facility for hastening his death by making us move him. Death coming sooner was not a bad thing. But I do blame them for making his last two and a half weeks on earth sad ones, and I'm angry with the incompetent nurse who should not be allowed anywhere near dying patients. This was not the ending that my dad deserved. Having witnessed the death of several people that went pretty peacefully, I was not prepared for a painful ending. He brought so much joy to this world. And I can't even begin to start missing him because I'm traumatized by those couple days. I keep replaying them in my head, and I'm having nightmares, so sleep is not a relief yet. I've never felt so helpless as I did keeping vigil. I know telling him it was okay to go was the right thing to do, but the way he'd moan a little louder makes me feel like he wasn't ready to leave us yet, and I hope he knows I was saying it because of just how much I loved him and wanted him to stop hurting, not because I actually wanted him to go.

I hope that, in the coming days as people share more stories about him, I can start to replace the last few days and years with memories of who he had been; that I'll remember all the love, all the silliness, and all the joy that he brought to us.

***

I'm scattered. Too many…all the very…does…not…compute. There are just too many thingsandstuffs in my head right now. I'm a little – okay, well, maybe very – useless right now. So if this seems a little muddled, be patient.

Honestly, I'm better than I thought I'd be following my dad's death. Most moments, I'm totally fine. When you've been grieving and losing pieces of someone for over seven years, you've already covered a lot of grieving ground by the time they finally die. Really, the only thing I've *just* lost is his physical body. But having that physical body around meant that there was still the possibility that the next time I saw him, he'd have a moment of clarity and we'd connect. I could still hug and kiss him, let him know how much I loved him, and some part of him might still know and want and return that love. That hope is gone. And now he's just…absent. I feel a little like I've lost a child (disclaimer: I am not a mother, so I know what I feel cannot even begin to compare to what a mother feels losing an actual child, so please don't get angry at that statement). I've already grieved for his healthy adult self. Now I'm grieving for the innocent, defenseless child he had become. It was our duty to take care of him, to advocate for him, the way you would for a child.

I got used to it. I got used to worrying about him and what the future held. I got used to hoping for a smile or a look of recognition. I got used to the pain I'd get at the mention of dementia. I got used to saying, "My dad has dementia." I got used to that being a huge part of who I am. It's part of my identity. And now that's over. I'm not quite sure who to be now. I mean, I'm still *me*. I know who I am, but now suddenly something is missing. Absent.

I used to see things that reminded me of him and that felt like it was him saying hello. Like a lucky penny or a train whistle. I keep expecting to see something like that that makes me feel like he's still here with me, somehow, but I haven't since that first day after he died. He's just absent.

A part of me believes in reincarnation. A part of me believes in soul mates (of the unromantic kind). A part of me believes we had a special connection like that. Which, I suppose, is why I expected to feel like he hadn't really left me, like he'd visit. But I haven't felt anything like that. His absence is sharp, stark, brutal, unforgiving. It doesn't make the heart grow fonder. It turns it cold and shuts it down. When I say something like how sad I am that he'll never get to see and be proud of what we've done with our business, someone always says something like, "Oh, but he *does* know." They say it with such assurance. I wish I had that faith. But I *don't* know. We went out to our property south of Raleigh and it was the first time I didn't hear a train whistle in the distance while I was out there. I dreaded hearing it because I thought it would make me sad, but not hearing it was even worse. It was just absent.

We're having a memorial celebration for him on Sunday. I'm hoping that will bring some comfort. I'm still having a hard time remembering who he was before the dementia. I've made a slide show and have watched it repeatedly, but it doesn't seem real. They're just pictures of who he had been a long, long time ago. When I think of him, I don't think of that. I think of the man in the dementia unit in various stages of decline. More than anything, I want to erase those images and replace them with my real dad – the one who was actually my dad, not my child. And even more than more than anything (yes, I know that's not a thing), I don't want to feel this absence.

What I wouldn't give for presence.

***

The memorial celebration on Sunday was beautiful, and painful, and wonderful. I have never felt so loved in all my life. I started the day with a radio tribute show for Dad with several of the other deejays, which was a lot of fun. Then lunch with friends from out of town. Then a quick nap and off to the memorial to get everything set up. We had way more people than we had anticipated, but the staff at the place where we were holding it were wonderful and brought in more chairs for us. Mom and I each spoke, then we asked for anyone else who wished to say something to speak. I've seen that go badly before, where everyone is afraid to say anything. But we cheated and sprinkled a few people in the crowd who were prepared to say something, and that got the ball rolling. It went on for about an hour. Seriously. People just wanted so much to express their love for my dad. And several people talked about how he had mentored them when they were younger. That theme kept coming up, along with stories about how he'd make people laugh. There were a few tears, especially during the slide show after everyone finished telling their stories, but overall, it was a powerfully positive moment in my life. Plus, we followed it all with a jazz jam session with his local-musician buddies, which was joyful and raucous and perfect.

My biggest fear had been that I would only remember my dad as he was with dementia, but the stories people shared at the service started to replace some of the traumatic memories from the last few days of his life. There was just so freaking much love in that room. My dad would have been so proud of all the lives he touched. I was proud for him.

I can't thank everyone enough for wrapping my family up in love this weekend. The wounds are starting to heal already.

***

I stopped for a milkshake today, and had a little flashback about my dad. After the sadness of the last couple days, I thought I'd share a little silliness with you. During the year that my husband and I lived with my parents, we had a schedule so that there was always someone around to keep an eye on him and so that we each still got some downtime. But keeping him entertained was a challenge, so sometimes when it was my turn, I'd take him into town for a treat like ice cream or a milkshake.

One of his favorite things was a peppermint milkshake. One afternoon, I drove him to town for said milkshake, and when they passed our shakes to us, I handed him his and turned around to grab a couple straws. In the ten seconds it took me to get the straws, he had upended his milkshake onto his face and swallowed almost half. He looked up, grinning, with a face covered in whipped cream and milkshake. He was like a five-year-old – just *covered* in it. And he was giddy. I hadn't laughed as hard as I did when I saw him like that in a long time. So I let him finish his shake (which took about twenty more

74

seconds) and then ordered a water to dip napkins in to clean him up since I couldn't take him into the women's restroom with me.

So now, whenever I get a milkshake, I will get my own giddy little smile remembering the abandon with which he enjoyed that peppermint shake.

***

This weekend, my mom came down to visit. Now that she doesn't have to take care of my dad, she can travel more, so we'll be taking turns visiting each other instead of me always driving up there. On Sunday, we got together with family for lunch. As we were sitting down to eat, Sebastian found two lucky pennies on his chair. No one knew where they'd come from, but for me, it made it feel like my dad was there with us. After lunch, a couple of the adults went out to hide Easter eggs for my cousin's toddler. To distract said toddler while they were doing it, I taught him how to hide heads-up pennies and say, "This is going to make someone verrrrrry happy!" Or, as the toddler said it, "Shashasha werrrry appy!" And so the tradition lives on.

***

So, you know the whole deal with my dad and pennies, right? Well, for the last few weeks, I've been finding lucky pennies in the road on my walks around the neighborhood. I've probably found about fifteen pennies so far. The front yard of one of the houses I pass is adorable. Very whimsical, full of colorful flowers and complete with a pink flamingo. These are definitely people with a sense of humor. So, when I found the first penny, I left it heads up on the post that holds their mailbox as I walked past, and said, "This is going to make someone verrrrry happy!" The following day, I found another penny on my walk, so I did it again. Before long, I had run out of room, so I started lining them up on top of the mailbox itself. I wasn't sure if they just hadn't noticed them or were choosing to leave them there. A couple days ago, as I went to leave another penny, I found them all gathered in a pile of the back of the post, which means they definitely know they're there, but have chosen not to remove them. Which means I love these people. I can only imagine what they must have thought when they first discovered them. I picture them counting them and scratching their heads. I'm betting they think a kid is leaving them there. When I walked past today, one of the residents, a man, was about to climb in his car, so I had to walk past the house and then circle back around and walk slowly so he'd be gone by the time I got there to plant the next penny. I felt so sneaky. Dad would have approved.

***

Last weekend, Sebastian and I went to visit my mom. While we were there, we went out to the cemetery to design the bench in which we'll be interring most of Dad's ashes. The salesperson kept trying to talk us into having all sorts of frilly imagery etched in, but we really just wanted it simple and clean. So it's just our names and dates on the sides, and lyrics on the top of the bench. After considering lyrics from several tunes, we settled on "See ya later alligator…" We used to say it to my dad when we'd say goodbye after visiting him and he'd happily say "after 'while, crocodile" in response virtually every time. I think it's appropriately silly and sentimental for our bench and makes me feel like there's a chance we'll see him again somehow, someday. Anyway, the next evening, Sebastian and I sat down to watch TV and immediately, up popped my favorite actor, Tom Hanks, saying, "See ya later, alligator" on a new sketch comedy show. I'm taking it as a sign that my dad approves of our decision.

***

I just got back from a 10 day trip to New England and back with my mom and S. As part of our trip, Mom and I decided that we were going to scatter some of my dad's ashes in the same waters that we had scattered his parents in. My aunt and uncle and cousin (and her family) all live in Hyannis Port, MA just down the street from the pier, so we asked them to join us.

They didn't currently have any boats in the water, so we just headed down to the end of the pier with our little baggie o' Dad. My aunt had very sweetly picked up some roses so that we could sprinkle petals, too, and I love that she chose red – vibrant and cheerful like my dad had been. We said a few words about who he had been, and I was blown away by something my uncle said. He said that, growing up, he had viewed the world as kind of a hostile place, and he'd battled through it accordingly. He said that it wasn't until a few years ago that he'd realized what an act of courage it had been for my dad to remain so kind and loving. It was an excellent reminder to me that I want to be brave like that; to forgive the world for its cruelties and look for the joy and hope where it can be found. There's so much beauty calling to us if we just pay attention. The trail of ashes and flowers washing away from us was so appropriate: life's most painful and beautiful experiences mixing and mingling and leading us forward.

After we scattered some ashes at the pier, we walked down to the breakwater where we used to hide pennies when I was a kid. My mom and dad and I would walk as far down as we could manage over the haphazardly strewn rocks to hide the pennies, and when we'd return the next year, we'd hunt for the ones we'd left the year before in the unlikely event that they hadn't been washed away by storms. And then we'd leave some more pennies in hopes that we'd either find them next year or give an unexpected surprise to fellow beach goers.

Life will throw all kinds of obstacles our way. It's our job to scramble over them and hunt for the little miracles tucked away, then leave some reminders for the people that follow behind us.

Dad, I wish you were still here so I could tell you that I'm paying attention and choosing to look for the light. #PenniesForNick

PART III

Chapter 7
Our Story in Paintings

One of the toughest things about this whole dementia thing was seeing it degrade my parents' relationship. They transitioned from spouses to parent and child. As the dementia killed off more of my father's brain, his understanding of their relationship was killed off with it. My mom became his mom, too. It was particularly hard to witness because I idolized their relationship. They were best friends and my dad absolutely doted on my mom. They were just really good partners in life. Of course, they had their problems because, let's face it, marriage ain't easy, nor is parenting. But they sure made it look easier than what I saw going on with my friends' parents. They balanced each other well, laughed at each other's jokes, shared the housework and building.

Watching that slip away sucks. Around the time we started noticing Dad's behavioral changes, he had to have his wedding ring that my mom had made repaired. It cracked and it no longer fit him properly. For their wedding, Mom had made their rings out of silver into which she cut two lines that crossed to create what appeared to be a bird, to symbolize their lives intersecting to create something new that could give them both metaphorical wings. Not long after Dad's ring had to be repaired, Mom's ring cracked beyond repair and she had to work with a jeweler to make a new one. As his disease progressed, she lost her new ring several times, but continued to find it. A few weeks before we moved Dad into a dementia unit, Mom lost her ring again and just could not find it. She instead wore a replacement band without the intersecting lines. Then Dad lost his ring again, never to be found. About a year later, Mom's ring turned up at the bottom of a bag, but it no longer fit and she chose not to wear a ring any longer. My dad was past the point of noticing. For their fortieth anniversary, Mom decided she really didn't want to celebrate, as the marriage was effectively over, despite my dad still being physically present. That was sad but understandable.

This painting is based on a photo of them as dirty hippies from early in their marriage. I love the photo, but I've used the dripped paint to symbolize the shroud that fell between them and over their marriage.

Dirty Hippies Kissing 8" x 12" acrylic, ink, and paper on canvas

Shortly after my dad was diagnosed, I got a tattoo of an elephant on my foot, because "an elephant never forgets." It's both a talisman and a symbol of dementia, and you'll see that I've used it in many more paintings about my father. The sheet music is from the jazz song, "Unforgettable," a song made most famous by a recording Natalie Cole made that included her singing to a track her father, Nat King Cole, had made prior to his death. One of my biggest regrets is that I didn't make more recordings of myself singing with my dad while he was alive. Throughout the series of paintings, I've used sheet music from my dad's gig books, so they were all tunes he used to play.

An Elephant Never Forgets 24" x 12" acrylic, ink, pencil, and paper on canvas

This was the first painting I did about my dad's diagnosis. I chose this elephant because it's young and looks like it's singing, and Dad had regressed to a quite childlike state and was always singing and playing music. He even had his clarinet with him in the dementia care facility and would play with musicians that came to visit. In the early years in the dementia unit, no matter what else was going on when I came to visit, he'd jump up when I entered to come give me a giant bear hug. He'd just light up. And he'd happily sing songs with me. The sheet music in the background of the painting is the song "Emily," which he used to play for me. In addition, I've added full color on the quarter notes to symbolize how the music he played and his memory were often fragmented – not "whole."

Happy Elephant Singing Emily 16" x 20" acrylic, ink, and paper on canvas

At my dad's gym, they had a wall of advertisements, and one of them was a picture of my dad doing yoga with the caption "The best is yet to come." When we moved my dad into the dementia unit and stopped taking him to yoga, my mom asked them to take it down because it made her too sad. This painting also speaks to my own fears that perhaps I'll share my dad's fate and get dementia, sticking close and blindly following where he leads in my efforts to be like him.

The Best Is Yet To Come 40" x 30" acrylic, ink, and paper on canvas

When I was little, the world was big and full of possibilities, and I would have gladly followed my dad anywhere, like in *The Best Is Yet To Come*. Now that I've gotten older and he has dementia, the world seems a little smaller (as is the canvas on which this is painted) and I had to start leading him. At one visit in his dementia unit, he was very distant and disconnected to the world, not really responding to my prompts or following where I led. I sat outside with him and cried on his shoulder. I told him I didn't want him to forget me and that I wanted his true self back. He started singing, "Que Sera Sera, Whatever Will Be Will Be."

Que Sera Sera 36" x 24" acrylic, ink, and paper on canvas

A continuation of the previous two paintings, and the smallest yet, this one reflects the stage where Dad had wandered off-track altogether. The moments where he seemed totally absent were more frequent, and I was starting to have to face what life would be like without him. The lyrics of the song "I Get Along Without You Very Well" include, "I get along without you very well, of course I do, except to hear your name, or someone's laugh that is the same…"

I Get Along Without You 24" x 18" acrylic, ink, and paper on canvas

As mentioned in earlier chapters, Dad developed compulsions as a result of the dementia. Some were innocuous, some were annoying, some were endearing. One of my favorites was that my father would go outside every morning, bow to the statue of the Virgin Mary that was in the back walkway area, and say, "Namaste." I also loved that the activities directors would have the residents practice writing their names, and when they gave him an A+, he started doing it on every piece of paper he could find. Then, for some reason, he would draw boxes around the signatures. In the painting "Compulsions," we see my father after he got hold of his roommate's razor and shaved off his facial hair, and he's surrounded by his own boxed signatures.

Compulsions 12" x 12" acrylic, oil, and ink on canvas

But as his connection to reality waned, so did his compulsions. Quite honestly, I sometimes missed them, just because they reflected a solid form of interaction with the world, and usually involved cleanliness. Plus, it was great having someone to kill all the stinkbugs for you.

We tried a lot of things to keep him happy and entertained – things that once upon a time would not have interested him and most likely would have annoyed him. But now he was happy to color in a coloring book or put together a puzzle and sing songs with me. With dementia, spatial perception gets screwed up, and patients often can't distinguish between things that are of a similar color. This is why you'll see a lot of toilet seats that are colorful in dementia care facilities. Residents often can't see a white toilet against a white wall. Similarly, the ability to color within the lines or put together puzzles becomes harder. Watching them color is like watching a three-year-old – fascinating when it's not your parent. When Dad was still sort of at the early-to-mid-level of his dementia progression, we tried entertaining him with puzzles, and he did pretty well, but it got harder and harder for him to do them. For Christmas one year, I wanted to get him some stuff to entertain him, so I ducked into a dollar store and looked at the kids' stuff – bubbles, puzzles, coloring books, activity books. And then I stood there stunned and realized that we had really gotten past the point where he could do those things anymore. I started to cry, knowing that even the simplest kids' puzzles were beyond him. This strong, intelligent, thoughtful man had been reduced to the mental state of a two-year-old in so many ways.

As this disease progressed, the story of our lives together and our relationship was lost bit by bit. The pieces that fit together for our own particular puzzle went missing in his mind, and his own identity went along with it. The way he gave me his own brand of Daddy hugs and kisses, dancing with me at my wedding: those things were disappearing, one puzzle piece at a time. I kept trying to gather them up and reassemble them, but at some point, I had to let go and know that the puzzles would never be whole and complete again, but that they're not any less precious to me. I can hold on to what remains and remember for the both of us, and know that even the tougher memories that were being made in his later years – the ones where he remembered my name, or laughed when I blew raspberries at him – are their own unique puzzles and should also be cherished. Or maybe they're all just additional pieces to a greater puzzle that encompasses the entirety of his life. And I'm lucky that I get to be the one that makes sure those pieces stay safe and are not forgotten.

Embraceable You 12" x 9" acrylic, ink, and paper on canvas board

Father Daughter Dance 12" x 9" acrylic, ink, and paper on canvas board

Similarly, the rest of his life could only be caught in glimpses. If you asked him a question about his life, he might or might not have been able to give you an accurate answer, and if he could, it didn't fit into any overarching understanding of the life he lived. With the painting "Peek-a-Boo," the viewer must lift flaps of the "Unforgettable" sheet music to view one piece of his past at a time, the way he saw it once the dementia had taken hold.

Unforgettable Peek-a-Boo 51" x 42" acrylic, ink, paper, and canvas

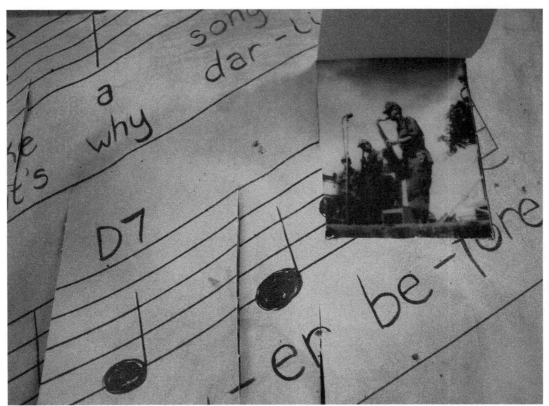

Detail of Unforgettable Peek-a-Boo

Detail of Unforgettable Peek-a-Boo

Interestingly, I find myself thinking of him in fragments, too, his life divided into songs. The music that shaped his life shapes my own. For example, the song "What a Wonderful World" will always hold special meaning for me because we danced to it at my wedding. I remember dancing with him and thinking about how long we had adored each other so. And in the last few months of his life, I had a chance to sing for him with some of his old band mates who came to play at his facility. The friend who had sung "What a Wonderful World" for our father daughter dance at my wedding attended our little concert, and we cajoled him into singing a tune, too. He picked "What a Wonderful World," and I cried while my dad sang a couple of the words with him and held his hand. It's strange how the things that happen later change how you see the things that came before.

What a Wonderful World II 20" x 16" oil, acrylic, ink, and paper on canvas

What a Wonderful World I 20" x 16" oil, acrylic, ink, and paper on canvas

Similarly, the song "Unforgettable," for obvious reasons, reminds me of my dad. He got me Natalie Cole's album *Unforgettable* for my birthday when I was a teenager, in which she sings that song along with a recording of her deceased father, and it was the first jazz vocal album I fell in love with.

Unforgettable 12" x 8" acrylic, ink, and paper on canvas

As the disease progressed, he became more childlike, giggling at stepping on frozen puddles, or blowing bubbles and doing arts and crafts, or watching kids' movies with talking animals.

Text reads: Perhaps the thing lurking inside my dad's brain all those years was really just youth. In his dementia, the burden of old age has been replaced with the joy of coloring in coloring books and stomping on crunchy leaves.

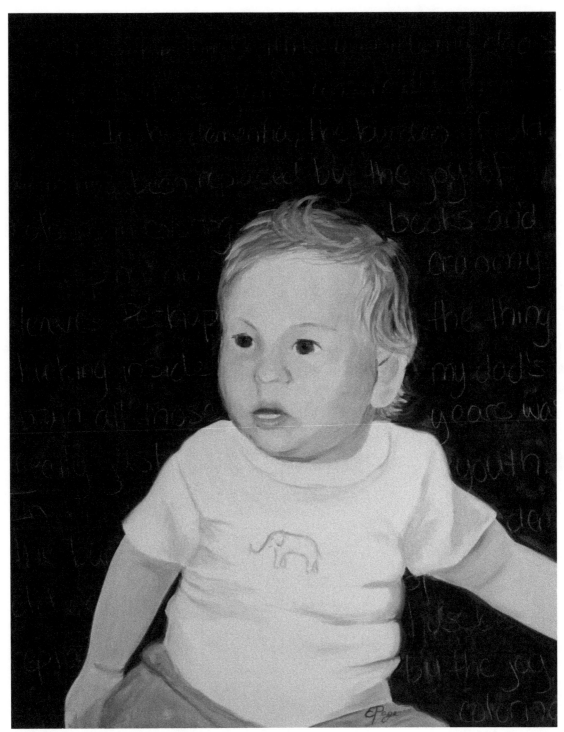

Youth 20" x 16" acrylic and pencil on canvas

While his early demented years were incredibly frustrating for us all, I can only imagine the terror he felt as he was still aware enough to know he was slipping. But eventually, he slipped enough that he was no longer aware that he wasn't sharp. Even though we knew he was becoming less and less himself and was becoming less tethered to us, there was some relief when he stopped being so agitated and scared.

Text reads: and in his later years, a second childhood found him, and he forgot that he had forgotten.

He Forgot 16" x 20" acrylic and ink on canvas

My dad loved to laugh. His laugh erupted quickly and easily, without restraint. And he made me laugh and laugh and laugh and laugh. And then laugh some more. And if I did something that impressed him, oh the proud-papa smile he'd give me. We were so incredibly lucky that, as his dementia progressed to the later stages, he returned to his loving, laughing self. So many patients with dementia become scared, angry, and/or abusive. I thank my lucky stars that that was not the case for him once he moved past the point of realizing he had dementia. When I hear the song, "Shadow of Your Smile," I think of him. The lyrics say, "The shadow of your smile when you are gone will color all my dreams and light the dawn." Yes.

The Shadow of Your Smile 18" x 18" acrylic and ink on canvas

This piece speaks to my fear that I will inherit the dementia from my father. The lyrics to the song in the sheet music "Dat Dere" are about a child asking her dad all kinds of questions, including if she can have "dat big elepant ober dere." There are so many traits I hope that I have inherited from my father, and in so many ways, I've strived my whole life to be like him. And in so many ways, I *am* just like him. Growing up I looked like him. We had the exact same sense of humor, the same taste in music, the same showmanship, the same ruinous need to make people love us, the same fierce love for our friends. And, for the most part, I'm proud of how much I resemble who he was. But now there's this thing that I could also inherit from him that I want no part of. I don't think it's possible to have a parent get dementia of any kind at such a young age and not worry that you're going to have the same future. When a parent is old and gets it, sure, you worry, but you can kind of rationalize and say that it's part of getting old. Not so when someone gets it so young. Your future was stretched out for another sixty years and that just got shortened by about twenty-five. That's scary.

I know you can't live your life worrying, because you could just as easily get cancer, or hit by a bus, or stabbed with a venomous platypus spur (okay, that last one is probably not all that likely), but still, your odds have just gone up if you have a parent with dementia. And dying from dementia really sucks, because the disease steals who you are many years before you die, and then you're just this shell wandering around and costing your family money and causing them heartache and maybe giving a few blessed moments of hilarity. So, if it's all the same to you, universe, I don't think I want dat big elepant ober dere.

Dat Dere 16" x 20" acrylic, ink, and paper on canvas

As your loved one starts to lose who you are, it feels like betrayal, even though we know it's not his fault. So we find ourselves practicing with him, as though we can drill our reality into him. We ask him, "Who am I?" We ask, "Who is your daughter?" We ask, "Who are you?" We ask, "Do you remember?" It's as though if we insist hard enough, we can will them into knowing.

Text reads: I do not want to remember you when you do not remember me. Or, more precisely, I want you to remember me. But, long after your mind has released the strings that tethered, through silver tinted memories, you to me, I will grasp wildly at those tenuous strands. I shall stand before you, insistent, willing you to recall my face and know my name. I will rip through those cobwebs, desperately hoping that, just for a moment, you will return yourself to me.

Remember Me 36" x 48" acrylic and ink on canvas

So much of my mood for the week after I visited my dad at the end of each month depended on my last visit with him. If he was more tuned in, I had an easier time of it. If he was more distant and less alert, I struggled. I think I feared that something would happen and my last moments with him would have been disconnected ones. And so, with each visit, I clung and pulled and tried to twist his attention back to me. More often than not, it didn't work. I hung on, with all my might, to those small moments that it did, terrified to let go and lose him again.

I don't think the need for your parents' love ever goes away, and I suspect that a lot of my clinging was my desperate wish that he could love me the way he used to. It's selfish. I know he did love me on whatever level he was currently capable, but it just wasn't the same. I tried every trick in the book – hurling songs he knew, family catchphrases, silly jokes he used to love – anything to get a look of recognition out of him. When I got an actual hug that felt real or a genuine laugh? Fugghedaboudit. That dangling carrot kept me coming back for more. I kept asking myself, at what point will I be able to let go of my need for him to recognize our relationship and instead just accept him as he is? Will I ever be able to stop trying to force him into it and accept that the disease is just too strong?

Text reads: I cling and I cling and I cling, but the disease chips away at him, turning him from me. How do you know when it's time to let go?

I Cling 4" x 12" acrylic and ink on canvas

My mom texted me that the activities director had taken the residents outside to enjoy the beautiful day. My dad had gotten up and wandered away several times, and on one of his return trips, he said to my mom, "I love you, Arlie." I still get teary at the thought. He not only told her he loved her without her having to solicit it, but he called her by the nickname that pretty much only he called her. It had been years since my father called me even by my own name, much less a nickname. He would tell me that he loved me, but he'd also tell the staff that, too. If I asked him if he loved me, he'd often say, "I do," but he would never say it without us soliciting it first. Occasionally he'd sing songs to me that we used to sing when I was a kid, and as far as I know, he didn't do that with the staff or other people, so to me that indicated some level of recognition, but he never called me by name anymore. There are no words for how much I missed him acknowledging concretely that he knew who I was and that I was important to him. I don't know why it should hurt so much that he stopped saying it. Intellectually, I knew that his true self loved me intensely and that it was only the disease preventing him from expressing it, but it didn't make it hurt any less to know that. There was an element of unrequited love to our relationship at some point (obviously not romantic love, but equally important), and it stung. Or rather it cut. Every time he failed to recognize me, it felt like a tiny little paper cut. I accumulated years of those cuts, and I felt like they were tearing me apart; like my skin was raw and the cuts were working their way into my heart.

Text reads: Watching a parent disappear in pieces to dementia is like getting a thousand little paper cuts: each one will not destroy you, but when you're covered in them, you begin to fall apart.

Watching your parent disappear in pieces to dementia is like getting a thousand little paper cuts: each one will not destroy you, but when you're covered in them, you begin to fall apart. Watching your parent disappear in pieces to dementia is getting a thousand little paper cuts: each one

Paper Cuts 20" x 16" acrylic, ink, and thread on canvas

I've struggled with whether or not to go into this. The daughter in me wants to protect my dad's dignity. The artist and writer know that my goal from the outset of this project has been to be honest, especially for those going through the caretaking journey. One of the most helpful things about being part of a support group is being able to say, "me, too." So with that in mind, let's talk about incontinence.

A couple years after he was diagnosed, Dad started having occasional bowel incontinence while he was sleeping. He was still with it enough to be upset at the thought of adult diapers, so we struggled with getting him to wear one at night, though he did eventually agree. But aside from that, he still had control over his bladder and bowels during the day. Not long after we moved him into the dementia care unit, he began going outside to pee. Luckily, the staff took it in stride, recognizing the only way to stop it would be to follow him around constantly, which he would not have appreciated. Then he started peeing on the carpet next to his bed. That wasn't so funny, as the smell was intense. He'd pee in his shoes, or walk through the pee-covered carpet in his socks, which made helping him put on his shoes particularly disgusting. The staff tried to cope by taking him to the restroom every hour, where he would dutifully unzip, rezip, and walk away without peeing. Five minutes later they'd find him peeing on the carpet again. We did eventually get him to wear adult diapers all of the time, but he would still drop trou and go when he wanted and where he wanted.

Then one day, I walked into his room and discovered two enormous piles of poop (seriously the size and general consistency of elephant poop) – one on the bathroom floor, one on the carpet. In front of the pile in the bathroom, someone had placed a "Caution Wet Floor" sign, as though that would have stopped any of the residents from stepping in it, or playing in it, or worse. Dad was standing beside his window playing with a train set, oblivious to the gag-inducing smell. I swallowed the bile that had risen in the back of my throat, and thought back to the song my parents made up when they were walking the train tracks many moons ago after a circus train had passed through. I walked around the pile on the carpet and over to my dad, took him by the hand and led him out of the room singing, "Don't step in the elephant poop, no, no, no, no, nooooo." I got my dad settled watching a movie and gathered the staff. They all apologized, no one fessed up to the sign, and several people donned gloves and cleaned it up. I went back out and sat with my dad and rubbed his back while watching the movie, quietly seething. I finally couldn't stand it anymore and gave him a hug and kiss and went out to the car to lose it. I screamed and cried and punched the steering wheel, surrounded by all the hatred I had for this awful disease. It sucked animalistic noises from my throat. The shame I felt on his behalf was crushing, and my anger at the staff intense, but mostly, I was mad at the disease for doing this to my family, to my dad, who did not deserve this.

The hardest part of incontinence for me, aside from the pain of knowing how humiliated he would be if he knew he'd reached this level, was the yuck factor. It made it a lot harder to hug and kiss him, because I was so aware that there could be urine or fecal matter on him. He had already started smelling a little off because of his chronic halitosis from the dry mouth caused by his meds, but the full-diaper smell when he eventually stopped realizing he was filling it made it worse. I hated asking the staff to change him when he needed it. I felt guilty, because I could have changed it (though it was a two person job) – heaven knows I did enough diaper changing when I volunteered for hospice – but it was different now that it was my dad. I couldn't bring myself to do it when I had the option of the staff doing it. I wasn't worried about seeing him naked – we were way past that point. But wiping his bottom…I just…it was too much. I hated going into his room, afraid of what I might find. I often held my breath when hugging him. My dad and I had always been snuggly, and I desperately wanted to maintain that, even while I desperately wanted to keep my distance. I reminded myself every time that he didn't get a lot of loving touch, and we all need that, and more importantly, that someday I would wish that he were still around to hug, smelly or not.

The sheet music is for the song my parents sang while walking the tracks over the elephant poop.

Elephant Poop 14" x 18" acrylic, ink, and paper on canvas

Each time my dad would phase down, we had to adjust and problem-solve to keep him happy and safe. We would get used to whatever the new normal was, and feel like we'd made peace with the new stage and where he was. But after each new peace offering and acceptance, the disease would charge ahead, breaking the truce and forcing us to adjust all over again.

Peace Offering 20" x 24" oil on canvas

Breaking the Truce 20" x 24" oil on canvas

With each step down in cognition and physical ability, we had to say goodbye to a piece of my father. Over the course of seven years, we said goodbye to thousands of elements of who he was, until, ultimately, we had to say goodbye to his physical presence, as well. There is a reason they call it the "long goodbye" and the "disease of a thousand goodbyes." Each goodbye feels like a death, so you grieve constantly, regardless of how long the journey takes.

A Thousand Goodbyes 30" x 30" acrylic on canvas

The way our friends and family have reacted is interesting. There are some who offered car rides when Dad stopped driving, or helped with his radio show; some who visited him faithfully in the dementia care facility, even travelling several hours to do so; those who were afraid to visit, but always asked how he was doing or sent cards; those who awkwardly but dutifully inquired about his welfare but didn't seem to listen; and those who disappeared completely. Of course, the ones who disappeared were a disappointment, but I can't really get angry with them. We all come to the situation with different fears and ability to handle hard situations, and not everyone is equipped to deal with something like this. When someone so young gets dementia, it's a blow to their friends that are the same age. Mortality comes knocking. And for the family, this is doubly so. Of course, I worry that I'll get it. Other family members were terrified that they would be next and worried that it was genetic.

There is no way to know why my dad got it when there is no familial history of note. We can guess that maybe he was exposed to Agent Orange in Vietnam (I have endometriosis, which no one in my family has, and there have been studies showing that daughters of Vietnam vets who were exposed to Agent Orange were more likely to get it), or the post-traumatic stress disorder he experienced after Vietnam did something to alter his brain. It's natural to want to find answers for why this happened to him when he was so healthy. If we can find something that makes his life experience or genes unique, it makes us feel better about our chances of avoiding it. But ultimately, I think it may just be some freak occurrence. He was just unlucky. And whether or not any of us get it comes down to luck, too. Something is going to get us eventually, and which disease or accident that is is largely outside of our control. So we can worry, or we can live. I have to admit that I do worry, and especially did early on, but I try to remind myself that if it's not this, it'll be something else, and I can't let fear control my life. So I live with the knowledge that I may not have as much time as I would hope, so I damn well better make the most of the life I have now.

Text reads: And so we ponder, why him? Why not us? Some flaw in his past that will make us immune to that fate?

Why Not Us? 16" x 20" acrylic and ink on canvas

As stated, I don't blame people for being afraid of my dad once he was diagnosed. It's a hard thing to stick by someone who has so fundamentally changed from who you've known them to be. And I know several people whose spouses had dementia and the children of said spouse refused to help. I decided very early on that I would not desert my father (or my mother, for that matter) like that. No matter how hard it got, I stuck by my parents, as they had always done for me. There's an elephant in a Dr. Seuss books who says, "I meant what I said and I said what I meant. An elephant's faithful one hundred percent." I resolved to embrace the elephant in the room in much the same way, promising, like the jazz tune "Come Rain or Come Shine" goes, "I'm gonna love you like nobody's loved you, come rain or come shine."

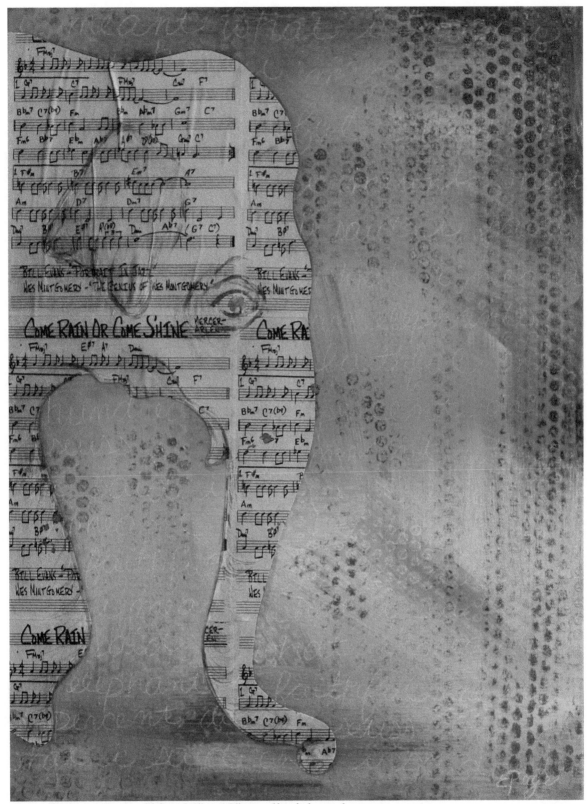

Come Rain or Come Shine 24" x 18" acrylic, ink, and paper on canvas

This is intensely personal, so please keep an open heart. I'm not really what you would call a believer. I was raised as a Christian, but wouldn't call myself that now. I've studied other religions, and none really hit the nail on the head, though some Buddhist teachings seem close, and since I don't have proof of anything, I guess what I'd have to call my thoughts on the afterlife are, maybe, "suspicions." Based on my readings and some compelling research on childhood recollections of past lives, I *think* reincarnation is one of the possibilities. I think we have a soul, which is energy, and that that energy can have different things happen to it when our bodies die. Sometimes it goes into some kind of collective, sometimes it gets reincarnated, sometimes it gets trapped in-between, and that's where reports of things like ghosts come in. These are just my thoughts, and I'm not solid on them since, again, I have no proof of anything, so I'm not looking for a religious debate here. You are welcome to believe whatever you want and I won't try to change your mind, this is just what feels true to *me*.

I also think that our souls are sometimes linked. I think soul mates might exist, but not in a romantic sense. In one life, you could be your soul mate's best friend, in another, an uncle, in another, a wife. It's a genderless thing and is fluid, but your lives will somehow continue to be connected. One of the reasons I believe this is that I had several instances of something happening to my dad up in Virginia (choking incident, pneumonia, injury, possible cardiac and stroke episodes) that coincided with me having a panic attack down in North Carolina even though I didn't know anything had happened to him. My dad and I have always been exceptionally close, and I think he could be my soul mate. Again, this is not a romantic thing. I think our energies are just linked somehow. I know this sounds very new age-y, and that's not generally my thing (I'm not going to join a commune and dress only in hemp skirts), but this has been feeling truer and truer as I've gotten older. I could be totally wrong and I fully admit that. But it helps me cope with life, so let me keep my delusions.

So, with that in mind, here's what this piece is about. I like to imagine that when my dad seemed less present in a moment, a piece of his soul was off wandering. Maybe crossing over to the collective for a bit, or checking in with another loved one. Maybe in those moments when I felt his presence even though he was far away, it was because his soul, or energy, or whatever you want to call it, really was there with me. I love the thought that when he seemed less with it, it was because he was floating free wherever his soul needed to be at that moment. As his brain deteriorated, his soul was less tethered to it and was free to wander. He was partially carried off to someplace else until he was carried off completely, eventually, to whatever the next phase for him would be.

Floating 24" x 24" oil on canvas

Most of us will lose a parent before we ourselves die, so it's pretty much the largest and suckiest club of which to be a member. Knowing that you're part of that group, particularly at a younger age, and that other people have gone through the same thing doesn't ease the pain of it. Each of our experiences with death will have shades of other people's loss, but it will still remain uniquely our own. And sometimes the emotional pain is so intense it feels like physical pain.

Text reads: The grief of losing a parent is ancient. I feel the weight of it settle around my shoulders, sink down into my heart, and encapsulate my gut. It's ancient, yes, but too new and too fresh for me to understand.

Ancient Grief 16" x 20" acrylic and pencil on canvas

The sheet music in the background is from a tune called "Old Folks," and it's my favorite cut on the album my Dad's band, The Red Hot Smoothies, recorded. We ended up using it for the background of the slideshow we played at his memorial celebration. My grandmother, Beatrice Page, was a novelist and a poet, and wrote a poem about her grandmother called "In Memoriam" that has always brought me comfort. An excerpt from the poem is stenciled on the painting:

In her ninety-fifth year
As the shadows
Were gathering
Her mind floated light
As a lily pad
On quiet pond

I love the peace that imagery invokes. It makes dementia sound softer, almost freeing, and certainly not scary.

Light As a Lily Pad 30" x 30" acrylic, ink, and paper on canvas

In looking for the silver lining, I remember fondly how we had to hold Dad's hand or link arms with him to keep him from wandering off or getting into trouble. I loved being snuggled up with him, connected physically. Those moments of caring for him felt good and safe, even if necessitated by the dementia.

Evening Walk 8" x 12" acrylic, ink, and paper on canvas

By the time he died, my father was almost unrecognizable. He was jaundiced and shrunken from days without food or water. It was hard to correlate the body in front of me with the parent I had loved. But maybe that's a good thing. Maybe that will allow me to divorce the image of his corpse from the image of who my dad really was.

And Then He Died 16" x 12" oil on canvas

The wonderful thing about how the dementia eventually progressed with my father, is that, as mentioned before, he was distilled down to a childlike state. Unlike so many other people with dementia who become cantankerous (this is being generous, some are downright nasty), my dad became innocent, bewildered, and loving, quick to hug and kiss whether he knew you or not. He loved to color, sing songs, and listen to Shel Silverstein poems. He would wait patiently while we fed him one bagel bite at a time. He felt no shame in his appearance, incontinence, or limited mental capacity. He was happy just to be – something most of us struggle to achieve.

Text reads: Elementally, my father is love. As the brain atrophies and tau proteins congregate, words and lyrics jumble and merge, faces and names become interchangeable, dates and events are lost and the body breaks down. Yet, he becomes more elementally himself, and he loves, and he loves, and he loves.

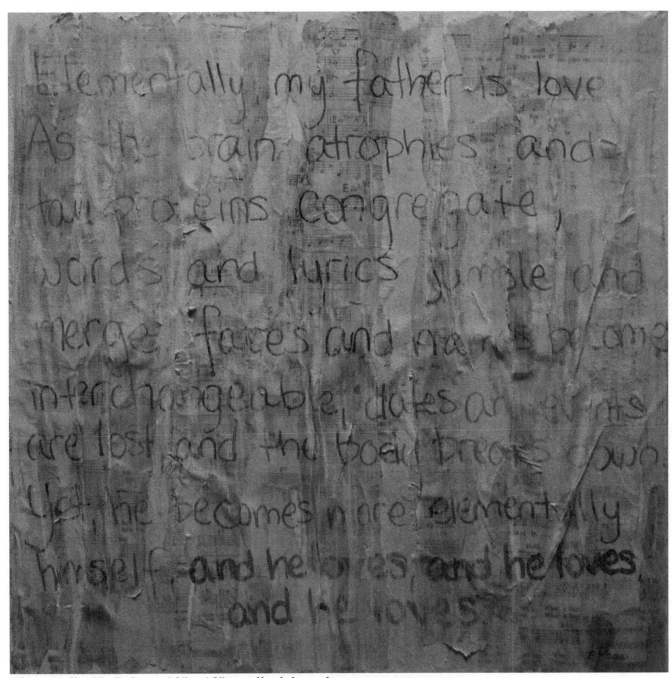

Elementally, He Is Love 18" x 18" acrylic, ink, and paper on canvas

Epilogue

The takeaway from my experience? Dementia sucks. You will be ripped apart by the humor and sorrow of it all. But there are opportunities for love and laughter. There are opportunities for you to live well and in the now. There are opportunities to forgive and rise above the pain.

You will fail, so go ahead and get out your sorrypants now (they're in the closet in between your crankypants and your fancypants, and they have pink hearts on them). Get ready to apologize. Get ready to accept apologies. You will fail your loved one because you will be put in impossible situations over which you have very little control. Your loved one will fail you because they have no control over what the disease is doing to their minds. Over and over and over again, you will feel inadequately prepared for the suckfest you've been handed. And over and over and over again, you will meet the challenge, get banged up by it, and move on to the next challenge – partly because you're stronger than you thought you were and partly because you have no choice.

You will miss opportunities to be kind. Forgive yourself. You will miss opportunities to be patient. Forgive yourself. Know that your loved one will forgive you, even when they can't express it or when they're saying quite the opposite. There is no way to get through this journey unscathed. But know that there will be more opportunities with other people where you'll have a second chance to be patient or kind because you've learned from the last time. You are better coming out of this than you were going into it. I know it doesn't feel like it most of the time. Most of the time, you feel battered and fragile and angry, but you have learned and will be a better person for it. You have the capacity to empathize in a way that you didn't before. So when someone else you know is going through this, you will know how to be there for them.

You will learn from this that now is all we have. Pay attention to it because tomorrow it'll be completely different. Say "I love you" early and often, and mean it. Set your life up to be what you want it to be now, not someday. Don't wait. Look for the opportunities in each moment to show love and forgiveness for all of life's little betrayals. And finally, know that you are not alone in any of this. Welcome to the club.

We Laugh, We Cry 20" x 16" acrylic on canvas

Acknowledgements

I'd like to thank the following people who helped make this book happen, either by helping me fund it, by proofreading it, or just by cheering me on and keeping me from going batshit crazy while I wrote and relived our journey through dementia. First, my mom (who helped proofread) and my husband, both of whom had to live through losing my dad along with me. I couldn't have asked for a better team of caregivers and friends. Your badassery is inspiring. You were hurting as much as I was, but you still supported me and helped me laugh. Thank you for offering insight when I got a little stuck while writing, and for believing that this wasn't a totally stupid and crazy idea. They haven't invented enough words yet to properly express the bagazillion (that's a bagillion gazillion for those of you who aren't mathematically inclined) "thank yous" I owe you. Next, Steve Gunter for forcing me to start a blog despite all of my insistence that I had nothing to say. To Kristy Berksza, for helping me embrace the ridiculousness in so many situations that might otherwise have broken me. To Aaron Weber for offering to edit the manuscript and then giving me confidence by telling me how little editing it still needed. And finally, a huge thank you to the following people who believed in me enough to contribute and order copies of the book before it was even written: Chris and Carole Page, Carter and Paul Catalano, Chris and Renae Page, Scott and JoAnn Wilson, Cassie Haggert and Alicia Orbea, Ellen Hogan, Holly and Alan MacEwan, Jesse Downing, Joe and Mary Catherine Miller, Kym Lord, Jolee and Thomas Faison, Laura Bridgewater, Laura Earle, Lynette Behrens, Mary Kyle Hughes, Joy Johnston, Louise Largiader, Michele Martin, Al and Michele Sinesky, Connie Brennan, and Will and Heather Bunn. Your support made me kick myself in the ass to follow through and get the book done, even when I wanted to run away from it to avoid the "ouch." I know I'm forgetting about eleventy-twelve people in this brief little acknowledgement, but I hope they'll forgive me and allow me to blame it on too much bourbon or something. Which reminds me: Thank you, bourbon. You're the best.

Listening Recommendations

In case you're not familiar with any of the songs featured in my paintings, here are some recommendations:

1. "Unforgettable," performed by Natalie Cole and Nat King Cole

2. "Emily," performed by Irene Kral

3. "The Best Is Yet To Come," performed by Ella Fitzgerald

4. "Que Sera Sera", performed by Doris Day

5. "I Get Along Without You Very Well," performed by Chet Baker

6. "Embraceable You," performed by Louis Prima and Keely Smith

7. "What a Wonderful World," performed by Louis Armstrong

8. "The Shadow of Your Smile", performed by Carmen McRae

9. "Dat Dere," performed by Rickie Lee Jones

CPSIA information can be obtained
at www.ICGtesting.com
Printed in the USA
BVHW061555020620
580778BV00002B/33